An Introduction

to the

Literature of the Bible

by

Stephen S. Carver

Kol Simkha
Publishing Company
Wilsonville, Oregon

An Introduction to the Literature of the Bible
By Carver, Stephen S.
Copyright © 2009 by Carver, Stephen
ISBN: 978-0-615-33004-4
All rights reserved.
Initial Publication date 3/15/2010
Second Edition 8/15/2011

All illustrations in this book are either commissioned works paid for by the author or are free images in the public domain.

The Scripture quotations contained herein are from the New Revised Standard Version Bible, copyright © 1989 by the Division of Christian Education of the National Council of the Churches of Christ in the U.S.A., and are used by permission. All rights reserved.

Acknowledgments

I would like to acknowledge those who helped to make the writing and the publication of this work possible.

First, I would like to thank students in my introduction to the Bible course and also Dr. Toni Pauls, Associate Vice President of Academic Affairs and Dean of the Adult Degree Program at Warner Pacific College. I am certain I would not even have begun this project if it had not been for the encouragement of the students and Dr. Pauls, who pointed out the need for a textbook such as this. Second, I would like to thank several colleagues and friends who read through early drafts and gave me guidance on matters of content. They include: Dr. Cole Dawson, Academic Vice President of Warner Pacific College; Dr. John Johnson, Professor of Missions and Chair of the Religion and Christian Ministries Department at Warner Pacific College; and Jarod Jacobs, Academic Counselor and Adjunct Professor of Biblical Studies at Warner Pacific College.

Third, I want to thank James Willard Johnson whom I commissioned to create certain illustrations for this book, and Timothy Swart who helped with the design of the cover.

Fourth, I want to thank the editor of this textbook, Esther Swart, who read through several drafts, correcting errors and helping to finalize the last edition of this textbook.

Finally, I would like to thank God who has given me life and allowed me to serve others through my teaching and my writing. Life is good.

Dedication

I dedicate this book to Dr. Timothy Ryschon, who has been my best friend since I was three years old. It simply is not possible to overstate the importance he has had in my life, as a friend, spiritual mentor, and counselor. I would not be who I am today without his love and care. Thanks, Tim, my dear brother.

Table of Contents

Preface ix

Chapter One
    Studying the Bible 1
Chapter Two
    Formation and Canonization of the Old Testament 11
Chapter Three
    The Pentateuch 25
Chapter Four
    The Historical Books 59
Chapter Five
    The Poetic Books 79
Chapter Six
    The Prophetic Books 95
Chapter Seven
    Formation and Canonization of the New Testament ... 117
Chapter Eight
    The Gospels 127
Chapter Nine
    Acts and the Pauline Letters 139
Chapter Ten
    The General Letters 163
Chapter Eleven
    The Book of Revelation 175
Chapter Twelve
    The Bible and Theology 183

Appendices
    Appendix A: Hebrew Alphabet 201
    Appendix B: Greek Alphabet 202
    Appendix C: Old Testament Timeline 203
    Appendix D: New Testament Timeline 204

Selected Bibliography 205

Preface

When I first considered writing this textbook, I hesitated, because I wondered how I could present the Bible in a fashion that honestly reflects the complexity of this literary and spiritual classic while at the same time make it accessible to a beginning reader or student who has little or no experience reading the Bible. Since there are 66 books in the Bible which are written in a variety of literary forms, it is difficult to comment on its contents without either drifting into detailed analysis which might be overwhelming to a new reader or into over simplifications that do not do justice to the complexity of the biblical material. So it is with some trepidation that I undertook this task, and I feel the need in my opening comments to state clearly what the goals of this textbook are.

One goal is to introduce beginning readers of the Bible to issues of authorship. There are debates among biblical scholars concerning who wrote each of the books of the Bible. While these debates can be very complex, they are presented in a summary fashion in this textbook, so that readers can be aware of the essence of the debates.

A second goal is to introduce readers to the basic content of each book of the Bible. Since there are 66 books in the Bible, sometimes readers of the Bible can be tempted to focus on only a few books, elevating their status above other books and utilizing those texts for the purpose of biblical understanding. However, a holistic understanding of the Bible based on knowledge about each book is important for the beginning reader, because this knowledge will help the reader to be aware of the breadth of biblical concepts. For example, while some books focus more on the need for a strict religious standard within communities of faith, other books emphasize the need for forgiveness and grace. There is a moderation of ideas within the Bible that is observable when the Bible is considered in its entirety.

A third goal is to introduce readers to the basic literary forms in the Bible. Like all literature, the books of the Bible were encoded into specific forms or genres reflecting the ancient cultures during the time that the Bible was written. While some aspects of those literary forms are found in contemporary literature, other aspects are unique to the biblical literary forms. In order for readers to be able to interpret and understand the various books of the Bible, it is important for them to know the rules of interpretation embedded within an understanding of the main literary forms.

A fourth goal is to introduce the readers of the Bible to how the Bible developed over time and how the Bible, as a book in its own right, contains themes that permeate most of the books in the Bible. The Bible did not simply appear in a moment of time, but it is the end result of many years of reflection and even debate within communities of faith which were interested in preserving a record of ideas and religious experiences that helped to shape their spiritual identities. As such, the Bible reflects deep spiritual convictions about important religious concepts, including thoughts about God, humanity, and eternal life.

As readers consider the issues of authorship, content, and literary forms of the books of the Bible as presented in this textbook, it is my hope that they will be able to encounter the sacred text more productively, as they develop an interpretive foundation upon which can be built a lifetime of biblical learning.

Chapter 1
Studying the Bible

THE Bible is one of the most studied documents in the history of humanity. Some read the Bible because they have an interest in the ancient world of the Middle East, while others read it because they believe it guides them toward a deeper faith in God. Regardless of the reasons why people study the Bible, one thing is clear. When it comes to studying this ancient text, it is not an easy task. Why is that so?

One reason the Bible is difficult to understand is that it reflects the mindset of people who lived in a world much different from our own. The normal day of the common person in the ancient world was one of a struggle for survival. Much of what the contemporary reader takes for granted in terms of food, clothing, housing, and safety simply were not available in the ancient world.

For example, ancient people had to invest enormous energy in the acquisition of food. Most ancient people did not buy their food, but they produced it or gathered it. Animals had to be killed and butchered before meat could be cooked and eaten. Many people in the ancient world tended flocks of sheep from which they obtained meat and wool, and they herded flocks of goats from which they gained milk and meat. Fruits and vegetables were grown in large gardens intended to produce enough for a whole year. While many regions in the Ancient Near East[1] did not have fertile soil or enough moisture for these crops to be grown, early civilizations were able to flourish in the region known as the "Fertile Crescent".

---

[1] The phrase "Ancient Near East" (abbrev. ANE) refers to ancient civilizations located in the area currently known as the Middle East, which includes the nations of Iran, Iraq, Syria, Lebanon, Saudi Arabia, Jordan, Israel, and Egypt.

The Fertile Crescent

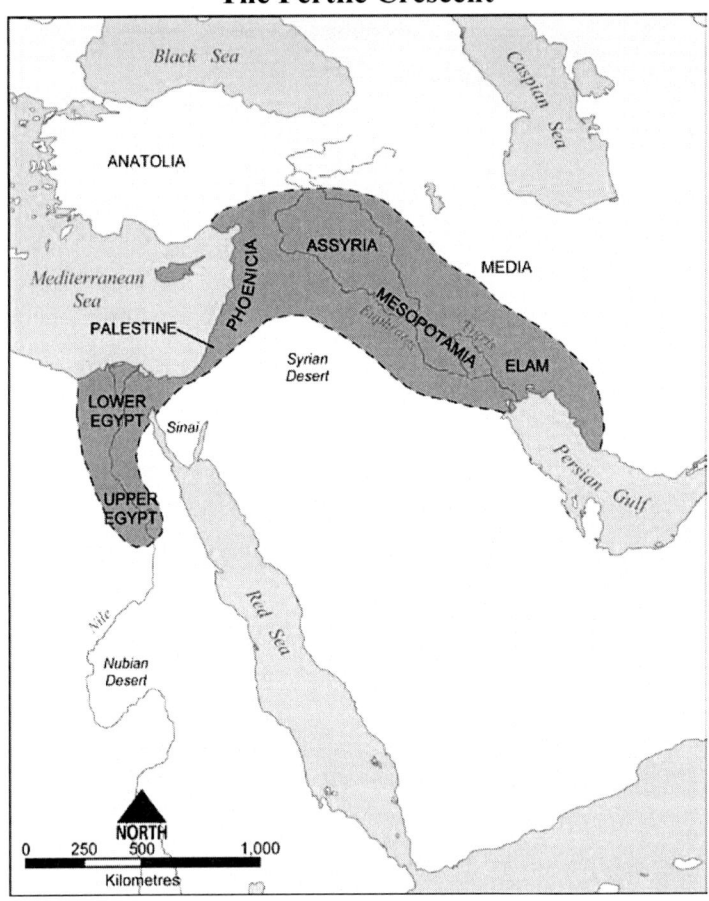

Stretching from the Persian Gulf in the east, continuing north through the area of the Tigris and Euphrates river and into modern day Syria, moving south along the Mediterranean seashore and eventually culminating along the Nile River in Egypt, this large area contained sufficient farm ground and water for civilizations to grow enough food to survive.

Wheat, barley, and oats were grown in fields specifically prepared for the production of crops. These fields had to be cleared of stones, plowed with oxen, and planted with seeds scattered by hand. Moreover, once the grain was grown, it had to be separated from the plants. The process of separating the grain from the rest of the plant involved threshing (i.e., beating the plants with wooden sticks) and winnowing which involved tossing the grain and the remaining plant elements (called chaff) into the air, so that the lighter plant material would drift away in the air, and the heavier grain would fall to the ground apart from the chaff.

Once the grain was separated from the chaff, then the grain would be placed into sacks, which would be stored in homes. Before grain was utilized for food, it was normally ground into flour, so that it could be mixed with water, thereby creating dough that was then baked into bread. Even water had to be hauled some distance from community wells, often by women who placed the water in large jars and carried the jars on their heads.

Just as most ancient people normally did not buy their food, they also didn't buy their clothing. Instead they made most of their clothing from animal skins or wool from sheep that were taken care of by shepherds, who herded them to water and grass and protected them from wild animals.

The processes for turning animal skins and wool into clothing were laborious and time consuming. Animal skins, known as leather, had to be scraped, cured in the sun, and treated with oil before they were cut into shapes that would be used for clothing. Wool fibers had to be sheared from sheep, washed carefully, and twisted into thread which would then be woven into garments.

Not only did the ancient people have to produce their own food and clothing, they also had to defend themselves from outside attacks. They lived in a violent world, where battles between warring nations and tribes were frequent and involved bloody combat with swords and spears. Being able to fight was so esteemed in this world, that eventually artificial battles were staged in arenas where men fought to the death for the pleasure of the crowds who came to watch and bet on their favorite fighters.

In order to provide protection against attacks from the outside, families joined other like-minded families and formed tribes, so that they could have a sufficient number of men of fighting age to protect them. Because they had to do so much for themselves, it was very important that they had a community to help buffer against the harshness of life.

When grandparents became old and feeble, they did not live on their own or in an assisted living facility, but they lived with their children. Children were not sent to daycare or school but were home everyday, being taken care of by their mothers, who taught them about life and how to survive. Given how harsh life was, it is not surprising that ancient peoples did not live as long as people do today. Therefore contemporary readers of the Bible need to be aware of the ***cultural gap*** that exists between themselves and the biblical text.

Another reason the Bible is hard to understand is that it contains passages which present customs, beliefs, and religious rituals that are clearly at odds with what is acceptable in the world today. For example, while contemporary religions don't offer animal sacrifices, the Bible commands animal sacrifices to be offered as atonement for sin. The ancient peoples believed the gods became angry when someone offended them. Therefore the gods needed to be given sacrifices, so that they wouldn't seek retribution against the offending human. In some cases, certain tribes even offered human sacrifices in order to appease the gods.

Not only are there strange ideas about religious practices in the Bible, but also there are concepts that seem to promote a very inhumane approach when it came to addressing conflicts. For example, most nations today do not believe genocide is acceptable, but in the Bible God commanded the Israelites to kill all of the inhabitants of the land of Canaan, so that they could establish a new nation later known as Israel. The commandment to kill the inhabitants encompassed not just the warriors but also non-combatants such as children. How could such cruelty be promoted in a book that is considered sacred?

While this is a hotly debated topic among scholars, a commonly accepted response is that ancient people had a much different view about religion than the contemporary view of religion. People in modern society are able to depend on protection provided for them by the national and local governments, but the peoples in the ancient world were not so fortunate. They didn't have policemen or a national guard to protect them. They had to fight for themselves and seek protection by invoking their deities. They developed special prayers in which they invoked their deities to attack their enemies and defend them from harm. The complete annihilation of an enemy would have been considered a tremendous blessing from a deity. Therefore, contemporary readers of the Bible need to be aware of the ***religious gap*** that exists between themselves and the biblical text.

A third reason the Bible is difficult to interpret is that it was originally written in languages much different from English. The writers of the first 39 books of the Bible (called the Old Testament by Christians and the *Tanakh* by the Jews)[2] wrote primarily in Hebrew[3] with a few

---

[2] As will be explained in "Chapter Two", there are a variety of names for this section of the Bible, depending on the religion and perspective that the reader brings to the reading of the first 39 books.
[3] The Hebrew alphabet is given in Appendix A.

passages in Aramaic. Eventually both of these languages utilized the same basic alphabet, and their sentence structures involve constructing ideas from right to left, instead of left to right as it is in English. For example, the first sentence in the Bible is as follows:

ha'aretz	ve'et	hashamayim	'et	elohim	bara'	bere'shit
הָאָרֶץ׃	וְאֵת	הַשָּׁמַיִם	אֵת	אֱלֹהִים	בָּרָא	בְּרֵאשִׁית
the earth	and	the heavens		God	created	in a beginning

As can be seen, this sentence is not only going the opposite direction of English word order, but also the subject and verb are in a different order from English. Instead of the subject coming before the verb, it comes after. This difference, along with numerous other differences between English and Hebrew, reminds the reader of the Old Testament that translations, as helpful as they are, can only capture some of what is being communicated in this ancient text.

The same issue arises when it comes to the study of the New Testament. Originally written in Greek,[4] the New Testament also reflects a system of communication that is much different from our own. For example, consider this sentence from the beginning of the Gospel of John:

En	arche	en	ho	logos	kai	ho	logos	en	pros
Ἐν	ἀρχῇ	ἦν	ὁ	λόγος,	καὶ	ὁ	λόγος	ἦν	πρὸς
In	a beginning	was	the	word	and	the	word	was	with

ton	theon	Kai	theos	en	ho	logos.
τὸν	θεόν,	καὶ	θεὸς	ἦν	ὁ	λόγος.
the	God	and	God	was	the	word.

While Greek looks more similar to English than Hebrew in terms of the alphabet, it is obvious from the order of the words in the above verse that Greek uses a different syntax (i.e., word order) than English. In fact word

---

[4] The Greek alphabet is given in Appendix B.

order is not as important in Greek as it is in English. The Greeks were able to move words around in the sentence more freely, because their language utilized word endings or suffixes which tell the reader how the word is functioning in the sentence. Therefore, the contemporary reader needs to be aware of the ***linguistic gap*** that exists between the reader today and the biblical text.

Given the differences between the ancient world and the contemporary world, a reader of the Bible could legitimately wonder if there is anything in the Bible that applies to today's context. It was written at a time much different from our own, in languages few people know, and in an exotic place far removed from our world today. Therefore, how can a contemporary reader possibly come to understand what the Bible is about?

Part of the answer is that biblical scholars have worked diligently to make the Bible accessible to the contemporary reader. They have translated the Bible into readable English, so that we don't have to struggle through the ancient languages. They have researched the culture of the Ancient Near East (abbrev. ANE) and written extensively about their findings, thereby helping us to understand issues arising from their reading of the Bible. They have worked through the biblical text verse by verse and commented on difficult passages, so that we can read their notes in order to gain understanding about what these passages might mean. They have determined the literary forms in which the passages of the Bible were written and presented methods concerning how to read those forms. Moreover, they have provided all of this information in a variety of resources, many of which are accessible to anyone who is interested in studying the Bible. These resources include:[5]

1) Study Bibles which have introductions to every book of the Bible and footnotes providing commentary on difficult passages.

2) Bible commentaries which provide in depth commentary on all of the passages in the Bible.

---

[5] For a list of books in each category, see the bibliography at the end of this textbook.

3) Maps which demonstrate the geography of the Ancient Near East and how the names of regions and cities changed over time.

4) Cultural background guides which provide insight into the customs of the ancient people groups.

5) Bible dictionaries which provide essays on a variety of topics related to the Bible including essays on biblical cities, biblical concepts (such as "covenant"), and biblical customs.

Along with the tools indicated above, there are other resources that focus primarily on the literary forms in the Bible. This textbook is one such example. In the following chapters, the reader will encounter a discussion of the major literary genres which occur in the Bible and how those literary forms reflect the major sections of the Bible. Besides indicating the literary forms, the readers will also encounter brief descriptions of each book of the Bible along with some commentary on the formation of the Bible. In fact, the next chapter is about the formation of the first half of the Bible, called the Old Testament by the Christians and the *Tanakh* or Hebrew Bible by the Jews.

Chapter Two
Formation and Canonization of the Old Testament

BECAUSE the entire Bible has been translated into English and contemporary readers are accustomed to encountering it in its current form, most people are unaware of the complex history of how this book came into being. The Bible in its current form reflects a long history of development involving the participation of numerous individuals in faith communities. Moreover, the books in the Bible were selected by these communities of faith for inclusion in the Bible based on certain criteria utilized over a lengthy period of sorting before the books of the Bible were declared authoritative for matters of belief and practice.

Meaning of the Word "Canon"

The process that books went through in order to be declared authoritative in the lives of believers is the process of canonization. The word "canon" is based on the Greek word *kanon* which goes back to a Hebrew word *qaneh*.[1] The Hebrew word refers to a reed or stalk that was broken off and utilized for measuring objects. As the word was altered and utilized in the Greek language, it took on the meaning of an "authoritative list", and this became its base meaning in the English version of the word as it has been applied to the Bible.

For those who have grown accustomed to reading the Bible in its current form, it is hard to imagine a time before the books of the Bible were written and collected into two distinct sets: the books in the Old Testament and the books in the New Testament. However, both sets of books (39 books in the Old Testament and 27 books in the New Testament) went through a lengthy period of formation before the books were selected for canonization or inclusion into the Scripture. Even the

---

[1] F.F. Bruce, *The Canon of Scripture* (Downers Grove, Illinois: Intervarsity Press, 1988), 17.

titles for these main sections reflect a time of change and development within the ancient community of faith.

Origin of the Title "Old Testament"

The 39 books in the first section of the Bible have been called the Old Testament by Christians. Why do they refer to these books in this manner? Have these 39 books always been referred to in this way? Actually, they have not. According to the Gospels, Jesus referred to the Old Testament simply as "the Scripture". Moreover, his people, the Jews, believed that these 39 books were "The Bible" in its entirety. So why did the Christians choose to re-title this collection the "Old Testament"?

Contrary to popular opinion, the word "testament" is not used to imply the concept of testimony as one might reasonably guess, but rather it connotes the concept of "covenant". Etymologically, the English word "testament" is a translation of the Latin word *testamentum*, which means "covenant". A covenant in the biblical sense refers to a deal or agreement between two parties in order to settle a dispute. In the Bible, covenants were established in order to create a relationship between God and His people. There are several covenants referred to in the Old Testament, and there is one covenant referred to in the New Testament. As the names of these two testaments imply, there is a tension between the relationship God had with the Israelites in the Old Testament and the relationship God had with Jews and Gentiles as described in the New Testament.

Built upon God's covenant with Abraham, the primary covenant in the Old Testament is the Mosaic covenant. Consisting of 613 laws which address a number of issues from food laws to civil codes, the Mosaic covenant was the constitution for the people of Israel, helping them to establish a stable nation. However, the writers of the documents later gathered into the collection of 27 books called the New Testament maintained that the requirements of the Mosaic covenant were rendered invalid by a new covenant which involved having faith in Jesus whom they believed created a new relationship between God and all humanity. Therefore, the writers of the documents in the New Testament maintained that the 39 books accepted as authoritative by the Jewish people were not as important as the 27 books they composed. Hence, the collection of 39 books was called "old" and the collection of 27 books was called "new" by Christians.

Formation of Traditions

While the above commentary hopefully provides the reader of the Bible with some understanding of the difference between the two testaments, it does not address how the first collection of 39 books came into being. An examination of the history of the development of the Old Testament reveals that the communities of faith reflected in the first 39 books of the Bible were spread out over a long period of time, perhaps as much as 1500 years.[2] Moreover, most biblical scholars contend that certain portions of the Old Testament were not written down at the time when the events mentioned in those portions actually happened. Rather, these portions were transmitted orally, perhaps for several generations before they were finally written down. This view has been problematic for religiously conservative scholars who are uncomfortable with the idea that aspects of the Bible might have been inaccurately communicated due to faulty memories.

However, other scholars have responded by noting that ancient communities relied heavily upon elders or shamans (i.e., religious leaders) to memorize accurately the traditions of their ancestors and communicate those traditions faithfully to subsequent generations. This seems very unusual to the contemporary reader of the Bible, because in modern society information is readily accessible through books and the internet. However, the ancients did not rely on the written word and in fact were suspicious of it even when it became more available. The ancients believed anyone could write down a falsehood, but they believed falsification was less likely if the person had to memorize a

---

[2] The first community of faith referred to in the Old Testament is the tribe known as the Hebrews, led by Abraham whom scholars believed lived around 2000 BCE. Later books in the Old Testament, refer to the struggles of the Jewish people in the late 6th and early 5th centuries BCE.

tradition and then present the tradition in person, face to face, to communities which looked to religious leaders for truth.

Nevertheless, at some point even these communities eventually began to see the value of written communication. Just as ancient shamans developed their memories and their ability to chant the religious and historical traditions of their people, later on scribes developed their ability to write sacred texts accurately and make copies for people in their communities to read. The question then became, which traditions were they supposed to keep and which ones were they supposed to discard?

Four Periods of Sorting Traditions

Biblical scholars contend that there were several times in the history of Israel where the Israelites had to make choices concerning what to include in their religious history and what to exclude. These periods included:

Receiving the Law on Mt. Sinai. After the Israelites came out of Egypt, Moses gave them the laws reflecting the covenant they would have with God. These laws included the Ten Commandments which included the requirements that the Israelites have no other gods but One and that they make no images of their one God. However, the Israelites had just come out of a culture which made images of multiple deities worshipped by the Egyptians. Therefore, the Israelites had a decision to make. Which theological view would they follow? According to Exodus, chapter 30, the Israelites had a difficult time in making a clear cut choice. In this chapter we read about how after Moses had been away from the people for some time, they decided to build a golden calf and worship it. Even though they had already accepted the Ten Commandments in principle, they were not able to break away from the influence of Egyptian worship easily.

Beginning of the Monarchy: According to Exodus 19:6,[3] God's plan was for the Israelites to be a "kingdom of priests, a holy nation."

---

[3] The nomenclature of biblical references involves indicating the book's title followed by the chapter number which is separated from the verse number or

The implication of this plan was that the Israelites would have no hierarchy among them and that they all would be representatives of God to the rest of the world, serving as God's priests. As such they would not have a human king reigning over them; only God would be their king. However, after they had conquered the Promised Land and lived in it for several hundred years, the Israelites decided that they wanted a human king like the rest of the nations around them. By starting a monarchy, the Israelites created a new understanding of themselves which would have required a transition in their traditions concerning the role of a human king.

Fall of the First Temple: Several centuries after the Israelites began the monarchy, they faced powerful armies from the east in the area of ancient Mesopotamia, where modern day Iraq and Iran are now located. One of those armies was from Assyria.[4] The Assyrians invaded in the eighth century BCE (abbreviation for "Before the Common Era"),[5] destroying the northern part of Israel and gaining control over the southern half which was required to pay tribute to the Assyrians. In the latter part of the seventh century BCE, another great army known as the

---

numbers by a full colon. Hence, Exodus 19:6 refers to a passage in the book of Exodus located in chapter 19, verse 6.

[4] Concerning ancient Assyria, John Brinkman notes that: "Ancient Assyria was a kingdom located in what is now northeastern Iraq. The earliest inscription naming a ruler of Assur--the settlement after which the kingdom took its name -- was Shalim-ahum, in about 1900 B.C. Assyria is known for its military conquests in the area of southwestern Asia. King Ashurbanipal (669-627 B.C.) collected a large library of Mesopotamian literature at Nineveh. Archaeologists excavated this baked-clay treasure trove in the 19th C. A.D." (*The Oxford Guide to People and Places of the Bible*. Ed. Bruce M. Metzger and Michael D. Coogan, [Oxford University Press, 2001]).

[5] Traditionally scholars dated biblical events in relation to the year of the birth of Jesus. Hence, events prior to his birth were referred to as BC ("before Christ") and those after as AD ("Anno Domino", which is Latin for the "year of the Lord"). However, many biblical scholars today prefer using BCE ("before the Common Era") and CE (the Common Era), because it is now understood that Jesus was born before Herod the Great died in 4 BCE. Those who dated his birth initially were off by approximately 5 years.

Babylonians arose in Mesopotamia,[6] and this army conquered the Assyrians. After conquering Mesopotamia, the Babylonians swept across the Ancient Near East capturing Judah (the southern part of Israel) in the process.[7] Judah paid tribute to the Babylonians for several years, but eventually Judah rebelled. In response, the Babylonians attacked Jerusalem and destroyed the city, including the Temple built by King Solomon, the third king of Israel.

The destruction of the Temple was extremely traumatic for the people of Judah, because it was at the Temple that they performed sacrifices that they believed made it possible for God to forgive them. Moreover, they believed that God lived in the Temple. Hence, whenever they wanted to draw closer to God, they could do so by coming to the Temple.

Therefore, when the Temple was destroyed, they had some very serious religious questions to consider. For example, if the Temple was destroyed, then was God no longer among the people of Judah? Moreover, since sacrifices could no longer be offered, did this mean that God would no longer grant them forgiveness for sins? The documents that had guided their religious thought up to that time had to be weighed against the reality of the destruction of the Temple. A new theology had to be developed in which God's presence was understood as being mobile, not stationary. Since God was not connected solely to the Temple, God could move about freely and be among God's people wherever they might be.

Return from Exile: When the Babylonians destroyed Jerusalem, they forced many of the people of Judah to go back with them to

---

[6] Mesopotamia is the name that refers to the region between the Euphrates and Tigris rivers, where modern day Iraq is located.

[7] "Babylonia (pronounced *babilahnia*) was an ancient empire that existed in the Near East in southern Mesopotamia between the Tigris and the Euphrates Rivers. Throughout much of their history their main rival for supremacy were their neighbors, the Assyrians. It was the Babylonians, under King Nebuchadnezzar II, who destroyed Jerusalem, the capital of the Kingdom of Judah, and carried God's covenant people into captivity in 587 BC" (http://www.bible-history.com/babylonia/).

Babylon in Mesopotamia. The people of Judah were forced to stay there until the Babylonians were defeated by the Persians in 539 BCE. Led by King Cyrus, the Persians were located southeast of Babylon. They were more enlightened than the Babylonians, allowing the peoples enslaved by the Babylonians to return to their native homelands and to rebuild their main cities. Therefore, the people of Judah, then known as the Jews, were allowed to return to Judah and to rebuild Jerusalem, including the Temple.

The rebuilding of the Temple caused the Jews to reconsider their understanding of God and their religious rituals. For approximately 70 years they had survived without the Temple. During this time, they had learned to worship their God by reading the Torah, praying in the home, and being ethical in their behavior. With the rebuilding of the Temple, a competing view developed concerning their worship of God. Once again, the Jews had a place to offer sacrifices again, thereby prompting a return to a more ritualistic approach to God. The tension between religion focused on ethics and religion focused on rituals is evident in a number of passages in the Old Testament as will be demonstrated in later chapters in this book.

Criteria for Selecting Books

Given the above dramatic periods in the history of Israel and the wide variety of religious traditions the Jews had available to choose from, how did they ultimately decide which books to include in their collection of Scripture? Some biblical scholars contend that the selection of books was done in a non-systematic fashion reflecting the changing needs of the Israelites. However, other scholars contend that books were selected based on four main criteria, including: a) the book had to be written by a leader (i.e., prophet, priest, or political leader) or a scribe selected by a leader; b) the book had to be esteemed by the community of faith as a whole, not just a few individuals in the community; c) the book had to be in harmony with other books already selected for inclusion in the Scripture; and d) the book had to demonstrate evidence that it had been inspired by God.

Three Stages of Canonization

Regardless of whether or not criteria were actually used to select the books that were eventually placed into the Old Testament, it is accepted by most scholars that the process of the canonization of the books in the Old Testament took place in three distinct stages.

The first stage was the canonization of the *Torah* ("law" or "instruction"), which includes the first five books of the Old Testament. According to the book of Ezra, the entire Torah was accepted by the community of faith by the middle of the fifth century BCE. At this time, a priest named Ezra returned from exile in Babylon and came back to Jerusalem. In order to promote obedience to the covenant, he read the entire Torah to the Jews and translated it from Hebrew (the language the Torah was written in) into Aramaic, a language the Jews adopted from the Babylonians while they were in exile. The books in the Torah are: Genesis, Exodus, Leviticus, Numbers, and Deuteronomy. As will be discussed in some detail in "Chapter Three", the books in the Torah (also known as the Pentateuch) present the creation of the world, several events in the early history of humanity, the stories of the patriarchs of the Hebrews, and the life of Moses.

The second stage of canonization involved a set of books known as the *Nevi'im* (the Prophets). According to an ancient document known as the Wisdom of Ben Sirach, this portion of the Old Testament was accepted by the community of faith as canonical (i.e., authoritative) by 182 BCE. This section of the Old Testament can be divided into two main categories: the Former Prophets and the Latter Prophets. There are 21 books in the Prophets altogether, and they are as follows:

Former Prophets		**Latter Prophets**		
Joshua	2 Samuel	Isaiah	Amos	Habakkuk
Judges	1 Kings	Jeremiah	Obadiah	Zephaniah
1 Samuel	2 Kings	Ezekiel	Jonah	Haggai
		Hosea	Micah	Zechariah
		Joel	Nahum	Malachi

As will be discussed in some detail in "Chapter Four", the books in the Former Prophets present key events in the history of ancient Israel, from the conquest of the land under the leadership of Joshua (who replaced Moses as the leader) to the destruction of Jerusalem by the Babylonians. As shall be seen in "Chapter Six", the books in the Latter Prophets contain the utterances of prophets who attempted to guide the Israelites during times of national crises in the history of Israel.

The third stage of canonization of the Old Testament involved the section known as the *Ketuvim* (i.e., the Writings). There are thirteen books in the Writings, and they are as follows:

The Writings		
Psalms	Ruth	Daniel
Proverbs	Lamentations	Ezra
Job	Ecclesiastes	Nehemiah
Song of Solomon	Esther	1 Chronicles
		2 Chronicles

As the title implies, this section contains a miscellaneous collection of poetic, historical, and apocalyptic books. The poetic books include a book of devotion, a love song, several books of Wisdom literature, and a lament over the destruction of Jerusalem. The books of history include: a) an account of the great grandmother of King David; b) accounts of the reigns of the kings of Israel and Judah; c) accounts of the return from exile and the rebuilding of the Temple and the city of Jerusalem; and d) the account of a Jewish woman who became queen of Persia. The sole apocalyptic book (i.e., Daniel) foretells the rise of foreign nations who oppressed Israel for a period of over 400 years.

Different Approaches to the Old Testament Canon

Since the books in the section known as the Writings were not originally canonized in chronological order, Christians decided to reorder these books and place them into different categories. Moreover, in the early Christian church, several books were added into the canon. However, while these extra books (known collectively as the Apocrypha), were later canonized by the Catholic Church, they were not accepted by the Protestant denominations which later removed them from the canon of the Old Testament.[8]

Therefore, the number and order of books in the Old Testament varies depending on the religious community utilizing it. While the Jewish people have kept the original three-fold order of canonization (i.e., Torah, Prophets, Writings), the Protestants have created four categories and reclassified the books of the Old Testament into those categories, which include: a) the Pentateuch which contains the five books of the Torah; b) the Historical Books which contains the Former Prophets and six books from the Writings; c) the Poetic Books which contains five books from the Writings; and d) the Prophetic Books which contain the Latter Prophets and two books from the Writings.

Similarly, the Catholics also have four categories, but instead of calling the third category the Poetic Books, they refer to that section as the Wisdom Books. Moreover, as was mentioned above, the Catholics have more books in their Old Testament. They add four books to the Historical Books section, two books to the Poetic books section, and one

---

[8] In the 1500s, certain Catholic leaders believed that there was a need for a reformation in the church. These leaders, including Martin Luther in Germany and John Calvin in Switzerland, eventually broke away from the Catholic church and formed new Christian groups such as the Lutherans and the Reformed church. Because these groups "protested" Catholic doctrine and faith, they were later labeled collectively as Protestants.

book to the Prophetic books section. The differences among these three approaches are demonstrated below:

Jewish Bible	Protestant OT	Catholic OT
Torah	***Pentateuch***	***Pentateuch***
Genesis	Genesis	Genesis
Exodus	Exodus	Exodus
Leviticus	Leviticus	Leviticus
Numbers	Numbers	Numbers
Deuteronomy	Deuteronomy	Deuteronomy
Prophets	***Historical***	***Historical***
Joshua	Joshua	Joshua
Judges	Judges	Judges
1-2 Samuel	Ruth	Ruth
1-2 Kings	1-2 Samuel	1-2 Samuel
Isaiah	1-2 Kings	1-2 Kings
Jeremiah	1-2 Chronicles	1-2 Chronicles
Ezekiel	Ezra	Ezra
Hosea	Nehemiah	Nehemiah
Joel	Esther	*Tobit*
Amos		*Judith*
Obadiah		*1 Maccabees*
Jonah		*2 Maccabees*
Micah		Esther
Nahum	***Poetic Books***	***Wisdom Books***
Habakkuk	Job	Job
Zephaniah	Psalms	Psalms
Haggai	Proverbs	Proverbs
Zechariah	Ecclesiastes	Ecclesiastes
Malachi	Song of Solomon	Song of Solomon
		Bk of Wisdom
		Ecclesiasticus

(For the rest of the books, see the next page.)

The Writings	*Prophetic*	*Prophetic*
Psalms	Isaiah	Isaiah
Proverbs	Jeremiah	Jeremiah
Job	Lamentations	Lamentations
Song of Solomon	Ezekiel	*Baruch*
Ruth	Daniel	Ezekiel
Lamentations	Hosea	Daniel
Ecclesiastes	Joel	Hosea
Esther	Amos	Joel
Daniel	Obadiah	Amos
Ezra	Jonah	Obadiah
Nehemiah	Micah	Jonah
1 Chronicles	Nahum	Micah
2 Chronicles	Habakkuk	Nahum
	Zephaniah	Habakkuk
	Haggai	Zephaniah
	Zechariah	Haggai
	Malachi	Zechariah
		Malachi

Given the differences among these three major approaches to these books,[9] anyone who decides to study the Old Testament will need to make a decision regarding which canon to use. The decision of this book is two-fold. First, it is important to honor the original canonical order and the importance these books have in the Jewish community. The books in the Old Testament were originally written in Hebrew by the ancient Jewish community in order to glorify the one God who had guided them out of slavery and into freedom. Through good times and bad this community clung to its faith in this God and thereby laid the foundation

---

[9] It should be noted that there is another major canonical approach to the Old Testament that has not been mentioned. The Greek Orthodox Church also has a distinct approach to the Old Testament and actually adds a few more books than the Catholics. For a list of the books in this church's canon, see http://www.bible-researcher.com/canon2.html.

upon which great religions (most notably Judaism, Christianity and Islam) built their religious ideas. If the ancient Jewish community had not led the way, it is hard to imagine where the world would be today. It was the Jewish community that led the way out of pagan thought which was focused on the worship of idols made of wood and metal. Moreover, it was the ancient Jewish community that demonstrated that the way of the law was the pathway to human equality and freedom. There is no way to overstate the significance of what they accomplished.

Yet, for the purposes of studying both the content and the literary forms of the books of the Old Testament, it is the perspective of this textbook that the Protestant reordering of books is the most helpful approach. While maintaining the exact same books that were in the original canon, the Protestant approach has the advantage of classifying the books according to literary genre. Therefore, this textbook will be following the Protestant canon, and the first section of this canon is the Pentateuch, which is commented upon in the next chapter.

Chapter Three
The Pentateuch

AS was mentioned in the previous chapter, the first five books of the Bible were originally known as the Torah, and later these five books were renamed the "Pentateuch".[1] In Hebrew, the word Torah means "law" or "instruction". Because the word often is translated as "law", the first five books of the Old Testament have been referred to as the Law of Moses. The advantage of this translation is that it highlights the fact that the 613 commandments of the Mosaic Covenant are given in these books. The disadvantage is that the word "law" does not cover significant portions of the Pentateuch which are written in narrative form.

There are a number of stories in the Pentateuch indicating how a small tribe known as the Hebrews grew into a great people known as the Israelites. Moreover, there are several passages of poetry in the Pentateuch. Hence, translating the word Torah as "Law" is probably not the best choice in terms of identifying what is actually contained in this opening section of the Bible. Rather, it would be best to translate the word as "instruction". The stories, the poetry, and the legal texts were written to instruct the Jews concerning their history and their religious traditions.

Authorship of the Pentateuch

There are several theories about who wrote the books of the Pentateuch. Based on their interpretation of early Jewish and Christian sources, conservative[2] biblical scholars maintain that these five books

---

[1] The word "Pentateuch" is based on two Greek words. "Penta" means five, and "teuch" means book or scroll.

[2] The word "conservative" is used in this textbook as an adjective describing a type of Bible scholar who tends to take the biblical text literally and uphold its historical reliability. "Conservative" scholars tend to be theologically oriented, as they attempt to demonstrate the significance of the Bible for matters of faith

were written by Moses.³ According to the book of Exodus, Moses was chosen by God to lead his people, no longer known as the Hebrews but as the Israelites, out of slavery in Egypt into the Promised Land, which was known as Canaan at that time. Raised in the house of Pharaoh,⁴ Moses would have been taught how to write, probably in Egyptian hieroglyphs.⁵ Support for the view that Moses wrote at least portions of the Pentateuch is found in the Pentateuch itself. For example, consider the following passages:[6]

> And Moses wrote down all of the words of the LORD. He rose early in the morning, and built an altar at the foot of the mountain, and set up twelve pillars, corresponding to the twelve tribes of Israel.[7]

> Moses wrote down their starting points, stage by stage, by the command of the LORD; and these are their stages according to the starting places.[8]

> Then Moses wrote down this law, and gave it to the priests, the sons of Levi, who carried the ark of the covenant of the LORD, and to all the elders of Israel.[9]

---

and practice. It is important to note that there is no attempt in this text to prove or disprove whether or not scholars who take this approach to the Bible are right or wrong. Rather, it is the intent of this textbook to present the main ideas of conservative scholarship, so that beginning readers of the Bible will know what their options for interpreting the Bible are.

[3] In *A Survey of the Old Testament* (Grand Rapids: Zondervan, 2000), Andrew Hill and John Walton note that "Hebrew, Samaritan, and early Christian tradition all regarded Moses as the author or compiler of the Pentateuch" (p. 576).

[4] The word "Pharaoh" is a title used for the king of Egypt in the time of Moses. The Pharaoh was a powerful king who was considered also to be a deity by his people.

[5] A chart with Egyptian hieroglyphs is found on the internet at http://www.earthyfamily.com/Egypt/picts/chart.gif.

[6] Unless otherwise indicated, all biblical quotations are from the *New Revised Standard Version* of the Bible.

[7] Exod 24:4.

[8] Num 33:2.

As can be seen in the above quotations, not only do these passages indicate that Moses was responsible for writing laws that he received from God, but also he wrote down the accounts of the travels of the Israelites. Based on this evidence and the belief that God told Moses supernaturally about the creation of the world and how God raised up the Hebrew tribe (i.e., events that occurred before Moses was born), conservative biblical scholars contend that Moses, inspired by God, was the sole author of the Pentateuch.

However, other scholars, who are referred to as "critical"[10] scholars in this book, have challenged this view for three main reasons. First, they contend that it seems odd Moses would have referred to himself in the third person. Given that he was the leader of the Israelites during the time the events recorded in Exodus, Leviticus, and Numbers occurred, why didn't Moses refer to himself in the first person (i.e., "I" instead of "he") as he did in the book of Deuteronomy? Second, critical scholars don't believe Moses wrote the Pentateuch, because there are a number of passages in the Pentateuch referring to events which occurred after Moses' death. For example, in Deuteronomy 34:5-12 the death of Moses is recorded along with a eulogy praising Moses for his leadership. It is unlikely that Moses would have written about his own death. Also, there are several verses in the Pentateuch referring to a time when Israel had a king. Given that Moses' death occurred approximately 1400 BCE and that the first king of Israel did not begin his reign until approximately 1040 BCE, these scholars contend that it is very unlikely that the references to a king would have been mentioned in Moses' lifetime.

---

[9] Deut 31:9.

[10] The word "critical" is used in this textbook as an adjective describing scholars who tend to see the Bible more as ancient literature than sacred Scripture. Hence, they do not have as much investment in the historical reliability of the Bible as the conservative scholars do. However, that does not mean all critical scholars are disinterested in matters of faith. It is just that they don't anchor their faith upon the historical reliability of Scripture. Also, it is important to note that there is no attempt in this textbook either to prove or disprove the position held by critical scholars. Rather, their views are presented so that beginning readers of the Bible know what their options are for interpretation.

Third, some scholars don't believe a single author such as Moses could have been solely responsible for writing the Pentateuch, because a number of passages within the Pentateuch seem to contradict each other. For example, the opening account of creation in Genesis 1 indicates that God (given the Hebrew title *'elohim*) created the animals before humans; however the creation account in Genesis 2 indicates that God (given the Hebrew name *YHWH*) created Adam before the animals were created.

Given the above difficulties with the view that Moses wrote the entire Pentateuch, critical scholars have proposed several alternatives to the Mosaic authorship view. One alternative is the view that the Pentateuch was based on four written documents spread out over a long period of time.[11] This view is called the **Documentary Hypothesis**. According to this view, four hypothetical written sources were utilized by an unknown editor in the fifth century B.C.E. who composed the final edition of the Pentateuch. The four written sources are supposedly as follows:

Yahwist Source (abbreviated as "J"): Supposedly written in the tenth century BCE (i.e., 999-901 BCE), this document uses the Hebrew name *YHWH* for God,[12] refers to God in human terms (e.g., God walks among and talks with humans), and focuses on issues related to the southern kingdom of Judah. This source was utilized in the writing of portions of Genesis, Exodus, and Numbers.

Elohist Source (abbreviated as "E"): Supposedly written in the ninth century BCE, this document uses the Hebrew name *'elohim* for God,

---

[11] For a fuller discussion of the Documentary Hypothesis, see the *New Oxford Annotated Bible*, pages 4-7 in the Old Testament section.

[12] Some scholars maintain that God's divine name is spelled "Yahweh". However, in the Hebrew text, only the consonants of the name are given. The vowels that are given with those four consonants are either the vowels that are used with the Hebrew word *adonai* ("my lord") or *'elohim* ("god"). The scribes who copied the ancient Hebrew manuscripts did not give the correct vowels with the spelling of the divine name, because they did not want the readers to pronounce the divine name, so that they would not break the third commandment of the Ten Commandments (i.e., "you shall not make wrongful use of the name of the LORD your God"). In ancient Jewish custom, only the high priest was allowed to say the divine name on the Day of Atonement.

indicates that God communicates through dreams, and focuses on issues related to the northern kingdom of Israel. This source was utilized in the writing of portions of Genesis, Exodus, and Numbers.

Deuteronomist Source (abbreviated as "D"): Supposedly written in the seventh century BCE, this document presents Moses' final speech to the Israelites before his death. In this speech, Moses recounts God's interaction with Israel and expounds on the laws in the Mosaic covenant. This source was utilized in the writing of Deuteronomy, which consists entirely of "D".

Priestly Source (abbreviated as "P"): Supposedly written in the sixth century BCE, this document stresses the importance of obedience to the laws, indicates the genealogy of the ancient Hebrews, and focuses on the cultic rituals (e.g., animal sacrifices) of the Mosaic covenant. This source was utilized in the writing of portions of Genesis, Exodus, and Numbers as well as all of Leviticus.

While many scholars are convinced that the Documentary Hypothesis or some version of it is the most valid approach to the authorship of the Pentateuch, other scholars believe that there is insufficient evidence to support the position that written documents were the basis for the Pentateuch. Rather, these scholars contend that whoever composed the final edition of the Pentateuch relied upon a variety of oral traditions which eventually were written into short literary units, and these were utilized by an unknown editor who compiled them into the document later known as the Pentateuch. This theory, known as the **Oral Tradition Theory**, has the advantage of upholding the importance of oral traditions in the ancient world as well as the advantage of explaining how those traditions eventually ended up as written texts.

However, this theory, like the Documentary Hypothesis, does not take into account the evidence within the Pentateuch (noted above) that Moses was involved with writing the laws as well as the travel narratives of the ancient Israelites. Given the preponderance of evidence supporting Moses' involvement with the writing of traditions within the Pentateuch, it is the view of the writer of this textbook that another view of the authorship of the Pentateuch needs to be proposed.

There is little evidence that the stories about the early Hebrews were written down by them, so it is likely that their stories were communicated orally by subsequent leaders and elders of the tribe until the time of Moses, who lived approximately from 1520 to 1400 BCE. Also, it is very likely that Moses delegated some of the responsibility for recording the travels of the Israelites to some scribes among the people, whom Moses might have taught to write. Once they were taught how to write, the scribes could have written down the earliest traditions remembered by the elders concerning the origins of their people. If Moses did delegate the responsibility for the writing of significant portions of the Pentateuch, then it is not surprising that he is referred to in the third person in those sections. However, even if that is the case, then how does one explain the existence of ideas in the Pentateuch which clearly reflect a time after his death?

While it is the perspective of this book that a significant portion of the Pentateuch was finished in Moses' time, it is not unreasonable to assume that later scribes copying the text of the Pentateuch might have inserted comments reflecting their own time. The references to the monarchy in Israel would fit into this category. Also, it is not unreasonable to contend that certain laws might have been modified during the transmission of the text reflecting the changing needs of Israelite society. While many scholars following the Documentary Hypothesis see within the Torah various layers demonstrating different layers of writing that only evolved *hundreds of years after Moses' death*, another approach is to view the layers as reflecting the different needs of the community in different time periods *before, during and after Moses' time*.[13]

In the earliest years of the Israelite community, they were a nomadic tribe that required laws to govern disputes among tribe members. An example of such a law is the requirement to return animals that have gone astray, even if they belong to a neighbor who is hated.[14] When the

---

[13] Charles Kent, *Israel's Laws and Legal Precedents* (Hodder & Stoughton, 1907), 12.
[14] Exod 23:4.

tribe of Israel conquered and settled in the land of Canaan, laws related to land became necessary,[15] such as the law prohibiting the movement of boundary markers. Later, as the nation developed, it was necessary to have laws related to military service and the qualifications of a king.[16] When the nation was facing national crises due to the invasion of powerful foreign nations and it appeared that the nation was at odds with God especially in the area of economic justice,[17] the prophets encouraged care for poor that later became codified into law.[18] After the nation was conquered and taken into exile by the Babylonians, the community of the Jews shifted their focus to ceremonies and sacrifices resembling what they had encountered in Babylon, with the addition of an emphasis on holiness that arose from the influence of prophets such as Ezekiel.[19] The law was ultimately codified in exile by the priests who made certain that the emphasis on ceremonial law was spread throughout the Torah.[20]

---

[15] James Mays contends that Israel adopted Canaanite law in the areas of criminal, civil, debt and property law ("Justice: Perspectives from the Prophetic Tradition" in *Prophecy in Israel*, [Philadelphia: Fortress Press, 1987], 152).

[16] Mays notes that during the monarchy the laws were expanded to include taxation, appropriation of lands, and forced labor (ibid.).

[17] The developing state moved away from a landed tribal system to a commercial society, and this brought with it new laws of the state that were not just. The prophets arose to address this issue (ibid., 155).

[18] Kent noted that the ethical mandates spoken by Isaiah that helped to avert the Assyrians from completely destroying Judah were eventually supplanted when the Jews returned to Canaanite and Assyrian ideas (*Israel's Laws*, 31). In response to this development, the book of Deuteronomy was written by disciples of the prophets in hopes of returning Israel to the focus on ethics. The emphasis in Deuteronomy, then, is upon an elevated social conscience as Judah was encouraged to love God and love each other. Blenkinsopp goes in a different direction. Instead of focusing on the connection between prophecy and law, he contends that "in Deuteronomy the legal and sapiential traditions flow together" (Joseph Blenkinsopp, *Wisdom and Law in the Old Testament: The Ordering of Life in Israel and Early Judaism*, [Oxford: Oxford University Press, 1995], 118).

[19] Kent, *Israel's Laws*, 36-38. Samuel Terrien notes that sages, scribes, priests and prophets interacted with each other and influenced each other ("Wisdom in the Psalter", *In Search of Wisdom*, 53).

[20] In this regard, Kent maintained that "these priestly laws represent the bridge over which the Israelite race passed from the highly ethical and spiritual religion

While critical scholars contend the existence of such phrases and changes to the legal text constitutes evidence of the Pentateuch as a whole being written much later than the time of Moses, it is the perspective of the writer of this textbook that such an approach is unwarranted. The existence of layers reflecting later thought in the community of Israel does not negate Moses' role as the initial giver and writer of the law.

Taking all of these observations into consideration, it is the perspective of this book that authorship of the Pentateuch should mostly be attributed to Moses. Hence, the **Modified Mosaic View** of the authorship of the Pentateuch has several main elements. *First*, Moses wrote significant foundational documents that were the basis for four of the five books in the Pentateuch. Some of these texts were edited and then added to the Pentateuch while other texts were added to the Pentateuch with very little editorial adjustment. *Second*, Moses trained scribes to write. These scribes collected oral traditions about the creation of the world, the great flood, the tower of Babel, and the accounts of the Hebrew Patriarchs from the Israelite elders and wrote them down, thereby creating the book of Genesis. These same scribes were also given the task of editing rough drafts written by Moses concerning the travels of the Israelites and the various commandments of the Mosaic covenant. Portions of the books of Exodus, Leviticus, and Numbers are a product of this editorial work. Shortly after the death of Moses, the scribes added the eulogy praising Moses and Moses' final speech to the Israelites. The speech and the eulogy became known as the book of Deuteronomy. Hence, the first draft of the Pentateuch was finished approximately 1400 BCE. *Third*, subsequent generations of Israelites made copies of the original Pentateuch and added texts and made changes reflecting their own time periods. The addition of texts continued until the time of the exile in the sixth century BCE at which point in time copyists were instructed not to add or subtract anything from the received text. *Fourth*, except for a few errors by later copyists, the Pentateuch has been

---

of the pre-exilic prophets to the rigorous ritualism of the scribes and Pharisees" (Ibid., 43).

faithfully transmitted since the time of the exile. It is this version that Ezra the scribe read from in the fifth century BCE.

While the above theory seems plausible in light of the available evidence, it is important to note that this view is a *theory* like other theories of authorship. There is not enough evidence to state with certainty how the Pentateuch was formed.

Literary Forms in the Pentateuch

As was indicated in the opening of this chapter, there are several types of literature in the Pentateuch, including historical narratives, legal texts, genealogies, and poetry. The most prominent type is **historical narrative**. Historical narratives present the history of an ancient people by means of a story. Stories or narratives have four main elements that need to be analyzed, including setting, characters, plot, and point of view.

There are three types of *setting* in a narrative: temporal, physical, and cultural. The *temporal setting* of a narrative involves the time period in which a narrative occurs. For example, in the history of Israel, there was a time when leaders known as "judges" ruled Israel (approximately 1360-1040 BCE). The judges were mostly charismatic military leaders who delivered Israel from foreign oppressors. When a reader knows the temporal setting of a narrative, then the reader is in a better position to understand the historical background of the narrative. The *physical setting* of a narrative includes descriptions of items in the narrative such as the type of clothing worn by the characters in the narrative or descriptions of what the characters looked like. In other words, the physical setting provides the reader with a mental image of a particular scene being described. Unfortunately, the biblical narratives are sparse when it comes to descriptions of the physical setting. For example, even though Abraham is one of the most important characters in the Bible, the writer of the narrative in Genesis did not provide any commentary on what Abraham looked like or what color of clothing he wore. The *cultural setting* of a narrative involves customs of a particular time period which are distinct from contemporary customs. For example, in the book of Ruth (one of the Historical Books; see the next chapter), the reader encounters the term "kinsman redeemer", but very little description is given concerning what this term means. Therefore, the reader of the book of Ruth needs to do research on this term in order to determine that the phrase refers to the ancient Israelite custom in which a childless widow was encouraged to marry a relative of her dead husband, so that children could be conceived and raised in the name of the dead husband.

After establishing the setting of the narrative, the reader needs to analyze the **characters** in the narrative according to function. There are four types of characters. The *protagonist* is the main character in the narrative. The protagonist can be a good person or bad person. This character must be identified before the other characters can be analyzed. An example of a protagonist is the character of Abraham in Genesis 12-23. In this section of the Bible, Abraham, under the guidance of God, leads his tribe into a new land and numerous adventures. Once the protagonist is identified, then the reader can determine the roles or functions of the other characters. Some of the characters are *proponents*, which means they are supportive of the protagonist. In the story about Abraham, a key proponent is his wife Sarah who protects Abraham from harm and cares for him. Other characters are *antagonists*, which mean they are working against the protagonist. In the story of Abraham, there are several kings who make Abraham's life hard, even to the point of threatening him with death. They clearly are antagonists. Both proponents and antagonists are key characters in a narrative, but the fourth type of character is usually only in a few scenes in the narrative. This type of character is called a *foil*. A foil is a minor character whose function is to bring out the characteristics of the main characters. A good example of a foil in the story of Abraham is the character Lot. A nephew of Abraham, Lot consistently chooses the opposite of Abraham and ends up in trouble out of which Abraham often has to deliver him. Compared to Lot, Abraham is much more admirable in his decisions and activities.

The third main part of a narrative is the **plot**. The plot involves the segments or units of the plot and the conflicts of the plot. The units of a plot are portions of the story that communicate one idea of the overall plot. In some cases, the chapter markings in a biblical narrative are helpful for identifying the units of a plot, but in other cases, the chapter markings are too broad. A unit usually has a verse or several verses introducing the characters and setting of one portion of the narrative. For example, in the book of Ruth, the first five verses set up the first narrative unit by introducing the reader to the characters of Naomi and her two daughters-in-law, Ruth and Orpah, all of whom were struggling to survive after the death of their husbands. After this focalizer,[21] the events of the unit unfold as Naomi decides to return to her land, Orpah returns to her family, and Ruth decides to stay with Naomi. This unit ends with Ruth and Naomi arriving in Judah. This is the defocalizer,[22] and this unit can be titled "Ruth and Naomi arrive in Judah". Every plot has several narrative units, each contributing to the overall movement of the plot. In the case of the book of Ruth, after the opening unit in which Ruth and Naomi travel to Judah, Ruth went into the fields in order to glean grain that fell to the ground after the harvesters went through the field. While she was gathering grain for herself and her mother-in-law, she met Boaz, the owner of the field. Because she was a woman of character who was helping her mother-in-law, Ruth was admired by Boaz. The development of this attraction is the point of this narrative unit, which can be titled "Ruth meets Boaz". These two narrative units can be represented graphically as follows:

---

[21] A "focalizer" is a passage (usually one or two verses) which contains information about a new setting, new characters, or a new situation at the beginning of a narrative unit.

[22] A "defocalizer" is a passage that summarizes what has already occurred in a narrative unit. The terms "focalizer", "events", "defocalizer" are used by Robert Funk in his book *The Poetics of Biblical Narrative* (Sonoma, Calif. : Polebridge Press, 1988).

Ruth & Naomi Arrive in Judah

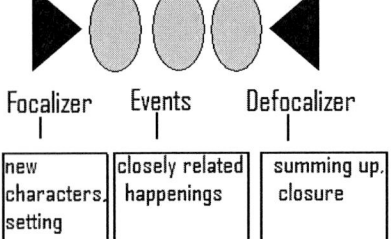

Ruth Meets Boaz

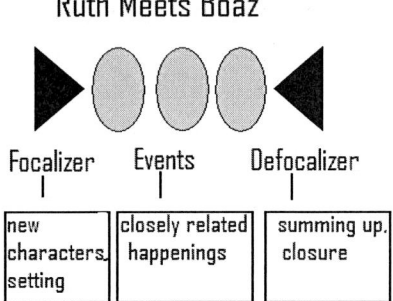

Concerning the conflict component of the plot, conflicts drive the action in the plot. As the narrative unfolds, the plot moves toward resolution of the conflicts introduced early into the narrative. There are three main types of conflicts. *Character conflict* occurs when one character is pitted against another character in the narrative. As was mentioned above, in Abraham's story there are several occasions in which Abraham had confrontations with kings. In one of those episodes, Abraham actually fought several kings in order to save his nephew Lot. This is an example of a character conflict. Another type of conflict is an *environmental conflict*. This type of conflict involves a character struggling against the elements of the environment. A good example in the story of Abraham was the occurrence of a famine in the land due to a lack of rain. The famine pushed Abraham to seek refuge in Egypt which leads to a character conflict between Abraham and the king of Egypt, who was known as a Pharaoh. A third type of conflict is *inner* or *spiritual conflict*. This type of conflict involves a character struggling with an inner moral dilemma or with his or her understanding of what God is requiring of them. In the case of Abraham, he had several inner struggles, including his struggle to believe in God even when God had not yet provided Abraham with a son who would carry on Abraham's name.

The last main element of a narrative is the ***point of view***, which is the perspective from which the story is told. In fictional narratives, there is only one point of view, that of the writer. All of the characters are figments of the imagination of the writer who creates them and guides them through the plot. However, in a historical narrative, there are three points of view. There is the point of view of the writer who has collected the material for the story and chosen what to include and exclude in the plot. There is also the point of view of the characters in the story. Historical narratives claim to reflect the lives of real people who lived in ancient times. So if the writer attempted to be accurate, he would have recorded how Abraham actually felt about the events occurring in his life. Furthermore, since there are references to God within many of the narratives in the Bible, the writer was also claiming to reflect God's point of view, which might be different from the writer's perspective and the perspective of the other characters in the narrative. So an analysis of the point of view of a historical narrative is more difficult to identify than that of fictional narrative.

Sometimes the plot of a historical narrative is disrupted by another literary form in the Pentateuch called a **genealogy**. Genealogies are often placed at transitional points in the narrative of the Pentateuch. The genealogies connect the characters of one account with characters of a much later time period. For example, after the account of the murder of Abel by his brother Cain, the first lengthy genealogy is given that connects the family of Adam and Eve with Noah, who is the next main character in the narrative. Along with providing a transition between stories, the genealogies also feature overt statements indicating the favored status of certain individuals in the list and/or a foreshadowing of the significance of a character in a narrative following the genealogy.

While the narratives in the Pentateuch connect together events by means of sentences linked together by conjunctions, another literary form, called **poetry,** builds in a different fashion, producing memorable verses rich in symbolism.[23] Poetic elements are scattered throughout the Pentateuch. The reader encounters them at key points in the narrative such as when an event is about to occur, an event is being celebrated (such as a military victory), or a main character is summing up prior experiences. Scholars divide poetic texts in the Pentateuch into categories, including songs, blessings and curses, and prophetic oracles.[24]

In the category of songs, there are tribal and local songs such as the song of Lamech, the songs of Moab, the song of the Well, and the song of Heshbon and Sihon.[25] Also there are Israelite national songs or fragments, such as the song of Miriam, the oath against Amalek, and the song of Moses.[26] In the category of blessings and curses, the reader will encounter Noah's blessing and cursing of his sons, Melchizedek's blessing of Abraham, the blessing of Rebekah, Isaac's blessing of Jacob, Isaac's curse of Esau, Jacob's blessing of Joseph's sons, Jacob's blessing and cursing of his sons, the priestly blessing of the Israelites, and the Ark Formula.[27] In the category of prophetic oracles, there are several passages, including the Balaam oracles, the oracle of Amalek, the oracle of the Kenites, the oracle about Assyria, Rebekah's oracle, and the Oracle on Moses.[28]

Productively reading the poetic texts in the Pentateuch involves paying attention not only to the form of the text, but also to its placement in the text. In order to understand the significance of a poem, readers are encouraged to consider what comes immediately before and after the poem, noting what the poem emphasizes about some aspect of the narrative. Moreover, poetry in the Old Testament has two key features called parallelisms and figures of speech which need to be taken into

---

[23] For commentary on how Hebrew poetry compares to other types of poetry, see T. Robinson's *The Poetry of the Old Testament* (London: Gerald Duckworth & Co. Ltd., 1960), 11ff.
[24] H.H. Rowley, *The Growth of the Old Testament* (London: Hutchinson's House, 1950), 37.
[25] See Gen 4:23f.; Num 21:14ff.
[26] See Exod 15:1-19, 21; 17:16; Deut 32.
[27] See Gen 9:25-27; 14:19f.; 24:60; 27:27ff.; 48:15f.; 49; Num 6:24f.; 10:35f.
[28] See Num 23; 24:20f.; Gen 25:23; Num 12:6-8.

consideration in the interpretation of poetic passages. Both of these features are discussed in "Chapter Five".

While genealogies and poetic passages play an important role in the Torah, the second most prominent type of literature in the Pentateuch after historical narrative is **law** or **legal text**. There are few legal texts prior to the story of Moses. Most of them occur within the context of the story about Moses, because they are the requirements of the Mosaic covenant, covering issues of sacrifice, hygiene, food, governance, festivals, tabernacle construction, and morality.

In ancient Israel, the priests were responsible for communicating the laws to the rest of the people. As the established religious class, the priests were consulted for civil cases[29] and were viewed as the guardians of the Law by the prophets.[30] The law brought with it legal consequence supported and enforced by the community should the law be broken. [31] This reality is attested to by the following biblical references:

> If a man steals an ox or a sheep and slaughters it or sells it, he shall pay five oxen for the ox and four sheep for the sheep.[32]
>
> If an ox gores a man or a woman to death, the ox shall surely be stoned and its flesh shall not be eaten; but the owner of the ox shall go unpunished.[33]
>
> If you ever take your neighbor's cloak as a pledge, you are to return it to him before the sun sets.[34]

---

[29] A significant aspect of priestly duties was "instruction in the laws" (Blenkinsopp, *Wisdom and Law*, 10).
[30] E.g., Mic 3:11; Zeph 3:4; Ezek 22:26; Mal 2:8-9. It is important to note that the task of interpreting the law shifted away from the priest and to the scribe during the exile (ibid., 16).
[31] Phillip Callaway notes legal institutions share the task of controlling human behavior along with family influence ("Deuteronomy 21:18-21: Proverbial Wisdom and Law" *JBL* 103/3 [1984] 341-352).
[32] Exod 22:1.
[33] Exod 21:28.
[34] Exod 22:26.

Also embedded into the punishments and legal obligations there were warnings related to God's concern that Israel should be careful to obey all of the laws lest they face cataclysmic consequences. If the legal consequences were not carried out due to corruption within the judicial system, then God would step in and punish the whole society. These warnings not only occur in the legal texts, but also they appear in wisdom and prophetic literature.

Scholars have long noted differences between two types of legal statements. First, there are laws with conditions called *casuistic laws*.[35] The civil laws in the Mosaic covenant are often in this form. For example, in Exodus 21:15, it states: "Whoever strikes father or mother shall be put to death." The opening part indicates the crime, and the second part of the sentence indicates the punishment. These laws mainly address unacceptable actions against people or property, indicating what penalty the offender shall pay. This type of legal statement in the Pentateuch has similarities to laws in other Ancient Near Eastern (ANE) texts, particularly the Code of Hammurabi,[36] who was the king of Old Babylon.

A second type of legal statement, called *apodictic law*, has the "you shall..." form. Some of the Ten Commandments[37] are in this form, including: "You shall not make wrongful use of the name of the LORD your God, for the LORD will not acquit anyone who misuses his name." Laws of this type are not given a condition or qualifier. They are to be carried out regardless of the situation.

For some readers of the Pentateuch, the laws are the most difficult to work through, particularly those which codify the details of the sacrifices. However, the existence of a substantial number of laws in the

---

[35] Casuistic laws are also known as case laws. Some scholars maintain that the Israelites adopted these laws from the surrounding culture (e.g., Artur Weiser, *The Old Testament: Its Formation and Development* [New York: Association Press, 1961], 55).

[36] For the text of the Code of Hammurabi, see http://www.wsu.edu/~dee/MESO/CODE.HTM .

[37] Exod 20:1-14.

Pentateuch demonstrates the importance of understanding this type of text. As the Israelites made the transition from slaves to a free people responsible for running their own nation, they needed laws by which to govern all aspects of their society. The laws were the foundation the Israelites needed to establish stability in the land that they were going to conquer.

Content of the Pentateuch

It is evident within these five books that the primary goal of this section of the Bible is to explain how the tribe known as the Hebrews became a mighty people who escaped from slavery in Egypt and prepared for their invasion of the land of Canaan, the Promised Land (later known as Israel).

Before the account of the father of the Hebrews (i.e., Abraham) is indicated, the Pentateuch opens with an account of the earliest humans and their struggles. The book of **Genesis** begins with two accounts of the creation of the world.[38] The first account demonstrates an orderly

---

[38] There is a debate among scholars concerning why two creation accounts are given in Genesis. Some contend that these two accounts come from two different sources, and that is why they are so distinct. However, others contend that they come from the same source and that the differences between the two accounts reflect a difference in emphasis, with the first creation account emphasizing the order of creation and the second emphasizing the relational nature of creation. Regardless what one chooses to believe about these two accounts, it is important for the reader to know that the creation accounts in Genesis are not the only accounts of creation in the Ancient Near East. Many ancient cultures had creation stories. For example, in ancient Babylon, there was a creation account called "Enuma Elish". It opens as follows:

> "When in the height heaven was not named,
> And the earth beneath did not yet bear a name,
> And the primeval Apsu, who begat them,
> And chaos, Tiamut, the mother of them both
> Their waters were mingled together,
> And no field was formed, no marsh was to be seen;
> When of the gods none had been called into being,

creation day by day as God spoke, bringing forth light, earth, plant life, animal life, and humans into existence. This account concludes with an exhortation to honor God as Creator by not working on the seventh day of the week. The second creation account focuses on God's care in the act of the creation of humans. God breathed life into the humans and placed them into a garden with two trees: the Tree of Life and the Tree of the Knowledge of Good and Evil. Humans were allowed to eat the fruit of the first tree, but they were prohibited from eating from the second. Tragically, the first humans disobeyed God and ate from the forbidden fruit, and they were driven out of the garden as a result. Most of what follows at this point in the narrative is more tragedy. A man killed his brother. Humanity became so wicked that God decided to destroy the world by flood.[39]

If it had not been for the obedience of Noah and his family, humanity would have ceased to exist. According to the sixth chapter of Genesis, Noah was a blameless man who was not like others of his time. In spite of all of the wickedness around him, Noah was able to hear God's voice which told him to build a large boat into which he, his family, and pairs of animals entered when God sent the flood. After the flood subsided, Noah accepted a treaty, called a covenant, which God offered Noah. As was mentioned in "Chapter Two", in the Ancient Near East, covenants were usually made between two parties which had a dispute. In order to settle the dispute, the party that had more leverage would make certain promises to the other party in return for obligatory favors to be performed by the second party. In the case of the Noahic covenant, God promised never to destroy the world by flood again. In return, God expected that humans, represented by Noah, would not commit murder,

---

      And none bore a name, and no destinies were ordained;
      Then were created the gods in the midst of heaven,"
(Translation by L.W. King; see http://www.sacred-texts.com/ane/enuma.htm)

[39] Hebrew culture was not the only one to record the flood account. Other Ancient Near Eastern cultures had stories about a great flood. One of the most well known examples of a non-biblical flood account is that of the Epic of Gilgamesh (see http://www.ancienttexts.org/library/mesopotamian/gilgamesh/).

would repopulate the earth, and would not consume blood.[40] The sign of the covenant was the rainbow, which demonstrated God's promise to the world.

Unfortunately, the Noahic covenant did not lead to better relations between God and humanity. Once humans became numerous again many years after the flood, God scattered them, because they attempted to build a tower that would position them to overthrow God. Not only did God disperse humanity, but God also gave humans a variety of languages. So God disrupted the wickedness of humanity once again, but this time without destroying humans.

While the earliest accounts in Genesis clearly show a creation continually at odds with God, the rest of Genesis demonstrates how a

---

[40] According to Genesis, prior to the flood, humans only ate fruits and vegetables. However, after the flood, they were allowed to eat meat. Since the vegetation on the earth was destroyed by the flood and it would take time for fruits and vegetables to grow back, God allowed Noah and his family, and hence all humans, to eat meat, but not with the blood, which was considered sacred. Blood represented life itself and was not to be consumed.

small tribe became God's chosen people. According to Genesis 12, God appeared to a man called Abraham (originally known as Abram), and God made several promises to him, including: a) to multiply his descendents; b) to give him the land of Canaan; c) to protect him from harm; and d) to bless others through him. In return Abraham was required by God to leave his extended family in Haran (modern day Syria), sojourn in the land of Canaan, circumcise himself and the males in his household, and be blameless before God. The promises made by God and the obligations upon Abraham constitute the covenant between God and Abraham. Moreover, the covenant made was binding on subsequent generations. It was not only binding on Abraham and his wife Sarah, but it was also binding upon all of his descendants, generation after generation. Hence it is not surprising to find the accounts of Abraham's descendants in the later half of the book of Genesis.

A key question that Abraham's descendants had to face was: who will lead the tribe? This matter was complicated by the fact that in the Ancient Near East it was not uncommon for a man to have several wives, and hence he would have a number of sons from whom could be chosen the next chief. In Abraham's case, he had to choose between his oldest son Ishmael whose mother was Hagar (a secondary wife known as a concubine) and Isaac whose mother was Sarah (Abraham's primary or number one wife). While Abraham initially preferred Ishmael and it was the custom at that time that the first born son would be the next head of the tribe, Sarah used her influence with her husband to assure that Isaac would be the head of the tribe.

A similar situation occurred with Isaac and his family. He, too, had two sons (twins) whose mother was Rebekah. While Isaac preferred the elder of the two sons whose name was Esau, Rebekah preferred the younger son whose name was Jacob. Following Rebekah's advice, Jacob was able to trick his father Isaac into giving Jacob the blessing for the first born, thereby solidifying Jacob's position as the next head of the tribe.

Even though both Isaac and Jacob were promoted ahead of their brothers, both of them had to overcome difficult trials. In Isaac's case, the trial involved almost being offered as a sacrifice by his father. According to Genesis 22, God ordered Abraham to offer up Isaac as a burnt offering, and Abraham was intent on doing just that, but God intervened at the last moment and had Abraham offer a ram instead of Isaac. In Jacob's case, he had to learn the hard way that living a life of deceit and trickery was not

acceptable. After deceiving his father and receiving the blessing of the first born, Jacob left the land of Canaan and traveled to the land of Aram (modern day Syria) in order to avoid Esau (who was plotting to kill Jacob) and in order to obtain a wife from their tribe of origin.

Upon arriving in Aram, Jacob encountered the tribe of his grandfather Abraham, and he met his future wife, Rachel. However, he was not able to marry Rachel immediately, because he didn't have a dowry to give to her father, Laban. So Jacob agreed to work seven years for Rachel. However, on the wedding night, Laban replaced Rachel with Leah, Rachel's older sister. When Jacob realized what had happened, he protested, but it was too late. He had already consummated the union with Leah, whom Laban wanted to be married before her younger sister. After an intense negotiation, Laban allowed Jacob to work another seven years, so that he could marry both sisters. Jacob agreed to this arrangement.

Not only did Jacob have children with the two sisters, but also each of the sisters gave Jacob concubines through whom were born several more children. Eventually, Jacob had twelve sons and one daughter with his four wives. The twelve sons of Jacob became the foundation for the twelve tribes of Israel,

as each son married and began extended families of their own. Eventually Jacob took his large family and returned to Canaan where he had to confront Esau, his brother. In preparation for this encounter, Jacob spent time praying intensely, and he encountered a heavenly being that he wrestled with during that time of prayer. Demanding a blessing from the heavenly being before he let it go, Jacob received his request as God told him that he would no longer be known as Jacob (which means "deceiver" in Hebrew) but as Israel ("one who struggles with God").

With the birth of Jacob's twelve sons, the issue of leadership in the tribe became more complicated. Before, one son was selected to become the head of the tribe, and the other son was sent on his way. However, it isn't possible to build a mighty nation of people if only one male is allowed to remain in the tribe. So choices had to be made concerning the next leader in a way that was convincing to the rest of the members of the tribe, particularly if a leader was chosen who was not the first born son of the chief. This was certainly the case in the last story in the book of Genesis where Joseph was selected by God to be the head of the tribe even though he was not Jacob's firstborn son.

Joseph's pathway to leadership was an extremely painful and difficult one. While he was the son of Jacob's favorite wife, Rachel, and Jacob greatly loved Joseph, Joseph did not have a good relationship with his brothers. This tension was compounded by the fact that Joseph had dreams in which he saw himself becoming the head of the tribe, and he shared these dreams with his brothers who grew to hate Joseph. Their feelings about Joseph led them to take drastic action against him. Once when they were out in the field tending their father's sheep, the brothers saw an opportunity to get rid of Joseph. After some discussion about whether or not to kill Joseph, they decided to sell him into slavery. The account of Joseph's life from that point onward is one of the most amazing stories in the Bible. After being sold into slavery, Joseph was taken to Egypt and sold to an Egyptian official. Because Joseph was so talented, he drew the attention of his new master, who placed Joseph over the other slaves in the household. Unfortunately, Joseph also drew the attention of his master's wife who attempted to seduce Joseph. In reaction to Joseph's repeated refusal to be with her, the master's wife accused Joseph of raping her. Apparently aware that his wife wasn't telling the truth, Joseph's master did not have Joseph killed as would have been expected at that time, but he did send Joseph to prison for several years.

Because of his ability to interpret dreams, Joseph was eventually released from prison and brought to Pharaoh who had troubling dreams he needed Joseph to interpret. Joseph interpreted Pharaoh's dreams which foretold of a great famine that was coming upon Egypt and the surrounding countries. In order to prepare for this time of famine, Pharaoh decided to appoint Joseph as the top official to oversee the collection of food before the famine hit. At the end of the book of Genesis, the story of Joseph concludes with Joseph's family coming to Egypt, Joseph confronting and then forgiving his brothers, and Joseph's father, Jacob, commenting on the future of his children.

The second book of the Pentateuch, the book of **Exodus**, opens with the statement that after Joseph's death new leadership arose in Egypt which did not feel obligated to Joseph's family anymore. According to this account, the Egyptians grew resentful of the favored status of the Hebrews (now known as the children of Israel or the Israelites) and decided to oppress them by making them slaves. The Israelites were forced to help build some of the great architectural wonders of ancient Egypt, including possibly even the pyramids.

The Pyramids

However, the forced labor of the Israelites did not hinder their numerical growth, so the Pharaoh ordered the killing of the Israelite male infants. It was in this context that Moses was born. Born of Israelite slaves from the tribe of Levi, Moses barely survived the edict requiring the killing of the male children. Able to hide Moses only for a short time, Moses' mother placed him in a basket near the shoreline of the Nile River where Pharaoh's household bathed. One of Pharaoh's daughters heard Moses crying in the floating basket, and she adopted Moses as her own. Raised in Pharaoh's household, Moses grew up in a place of power and luxury.

However, the day came when Moses rejected this life of privilege. Upon seeing an Israelite slave being abused by an Egyptian, Moses stepped in and killed the Egyptian. Moses then fled Egypt, going to the land of Midian. There he married a woman named Zipporah, and Moses became a shepherd for forty years. However, Moses was not destined to remain as a shepherd of sheep. According to the third chapter of Exodus, God had other plans for him.

One day when Moses was tending the sheep, he saw a bush burning, but it was not being consumed by the fire. As Moses turned aside to see what was happening, God spoke to him and told him that God had chosen Moses to deliver the Israelites from slavery and to bring them into a place of their own, the Promised Land.

After much reluctance, Moses left Midian and returned to Egypt where he confronted Pharaoh. Pharaoh was not impressed by Moses' request to release the Israelite slaves, nor was Pharaoh impressed by the miraculous signs that God had given Moses to perform in front of Pharaoh, including turning Moses' staff into a snake and back again, having Moses' hand become white with leprosy and back again, and turning water into blood. Pharaoh's refusal to grant Moses' request led to a series of confrontations between Moses and Pharaoh. In the first few confrontations, Pharaoh dismissed Moses and was not concerned when plagues came upon Egypt. However as the plagues became more drastic, the confrontations intensified, and a pattern for the confrontations solidified, including: a) Moses warning Pharaoh that a plague would come upon Egypt if Pharaoh refused to release the Hebrews; b) Pharaoh refusing to grant the request; c) God sending a plague on Egypt; d) Pharaoh begging Moses to stop the plague; e) Moses praying to God who then stopped the plague; and f) Pharaoh changing his mind and refusing to let the Israelites go.

Finally, Moses warned Pharaoh that the confrontations were coming to an end. A horrible plague was coming upon Egypt, and this would break Pharaoh. This plague involved the death of all first born in Egypt. Tragically, Pharaoh refused to listen, and the plague was unleashed upon Egypt. Instructed by Moses to sacrifice a lamb and use some of the lamb's blood to mark their doorways, the Israelites were spared the death of their firstborn, because according to Exodus, the angel of death saw the blood on the doorways of the Israelites and consequently *passed over* those households. The ceremonial meal eaten by the Israelites at that time became known as Passover, which became a Jewish holy day commemorating deliverance from slavery.

Overcome by the destruction that had been wrecked on Egypt, Pharaoh finally let the Israelites go, but after they left, Pharaoh once again changed his mind and sent his army after the fleeing Israelites. The final confrontation occurred at the Red Sea. According to Exodus, God parted the Red Sea, allowing the Israelites to escape to the other side, but when the Egyptian army tried to do likewise, God caused the walls of water to collapse, thereby destroying the Egyptian army.

After celebrating their miraculous deliverance, the Israelites found themselves in a difficult place. While no longer slaves, they didn't know what to do. They were in a desert with no food (except manna from heaven)[41] or water, and they were no longer in the structure provided by the Egyptians. The second half of the book of Exodus indicates that the Israelites had much to learn about being a free people. They needed to learn how to govern themselves, how to structure their daily lives, and how to defend themselves from enemies. Moreover, they were uncertain about Moses as their leader. Even though he had proven himself by leading them out of Egypt, he struggled to maintain control of the Israelites.

---

[41] According to the Bible, manna was a seed like substance that was like dew upon the ground every morning. The Israelites would pick up the manna and grind it into flour for their daily bread.

Since there were so many of them (probably more than 2 million) and they were so difficult to manage, Moses created a system of judges who would rule in cases of civil dispute and teach the people proper behavior. In order to establish this new system, Moses needed a code of laws that he could refer to. According to Exodus 20, Moses was given this law code by God. The first ten laws given were the Ten Commandments, and according to this account, these commandments were written on tablets of stone by God. The Ten Commandments are as follows:[42]

1) I am the LORD your God, who brought you out of the land of Egypt, out of the house of slavery; you shall have no other gods before me.
2) You shall not make for yourself an idol.
3) You shall not make wrongful use of the name of the LORD your God.
4) Remember the Sabbath day, and keep it holy. Six days you shall labor and do all your work. But the seventh day is a Sabbath to the LORD your God; you shall not do any work.
5) Honor your father and your mother.
6) You shall not murder.
7) You shall not commit adultery.
8) You shall not steal.
9) You shall not bear false witness against your neighbor.
10) You shall not covet.

As can be seen, the Ten Commandments focus both on the Israelites' relationship with God as well as how they were to treat each other. The two-fold aspect of the Ten Commandments is repeated throughout the numerous other commandments that are in the Mosaic Covenant. After

---

[42] The Ten Commandments are listed several times in the Pentateuch. The version quoted in this text is from Exodus 20:2-17.

presenting these commandments (and numerous others) to the Israelites orally, Moses asked them if they agreed to obey these laws and thereby enter into a binding agreement with God. They agreed wholeheartedly. The Israelites were to be a "priestly kingdom and a holy nation" to God.[43]

Unfortunately, the generation of Israelites fresh out of slavery had a difficult time embracing this vision for themselves. They rebelled frequently against God and the chosen leader Moses. The first rebellion is indicated in Exodus, chapter 32. According to this passage, while Moses was up on a mountain conversing with God, the Israelites built a golden calf and worshipped it. When Moses came down from the mountain and found out what had happened, he threw down the two tablets containing the Ten Commandments and broke them. Then he called on members of his tribe, the Levites, to kill the leaders of the rebellion.

Shortly after the rebellion was brought under control, Moses ordered the building of the tabernacle. The tabernacle was a tent structure consisting of an outer court where the sacrifices were offered as well as an inner sacred space which contained a second copy of the Ten Commandments. It was built to be the spiritual focus of the Israelites, who apparently needed a physical symbol for their worship. Moreover, it was used by God to guide the Israelites' journey through the wilderness. When God wanted the Israelites to stay in one place, God's presence (a pillar of cloud by day and a pillar of fire by night) would hover over the tabernacle, but when he wanted the Israelites to move, God would move the clouds or the pillar.

---

[43] Exod 19:6.

The Tabernacle of Israel

Along with the instructions for constructing the Tabernacle, the Israelites were also given a number of laws related to all aspects of daily life. Located in the second half of Exodus and throughout the book of **Leviticus** (the third book of the Pentateuch), these laws provided the Israelites with a constitution for a new nation, not governed by a Pharaoh or a king, but governed by the rule of law under the guidance of the God who had delivered them from slavery. There are a total of 613 commandments in this constition/covenant, covering such areas as civil law (what are the penalties for personnel and property disputes), food laws (what can and cannot be eaten), cleanliness laws (what rendered people unclean and the rituals they had to perform to become clean), sexual laws (prohibitions against immoral activities), disease laws (when to quarantine someone and how they could be restored), sacrificial laws (what was to be sacrificed to God and how the altar had to be prepared), priest laws (how the priests were to be prepared for carrying out the sacrifices), and festival laws (what were the special national holidays and what was supposed to be performed during those days). Located among these detailed instructions for the nation of Israel is one of the most profound commandments in the whole Bible, a commandment that Jesus highlighted in his teaching: "You shall love your neighbor as yourself."[44]

With the Tabernacle completed and most of the laws in hand,[45] the Israelites were finally ready to leave Mount Sinai and begin their journey to the Promised Land. According to the book of **Numbers** (the fourth book in the Pentateuch), God commanded the Israelites to invade the land of Canaan and make it their nation. However, the people were afraid of the Canaanites, and so they refused to enter. Due to this disobedience, God punished the Israelites by forcing them to wander in the wilderness for forty years. The generation of adults who came out of Egypt would not be allowed to enter into the Promised Land. They would die in the wilderness, and their children would be given the task of conquering the land.

While the account of the Israelites took a negative turn after they crossed the Red Sea and successfully built the Tabernacle, the book of Numbers does not conclude on that sour note. Rather, toward the end of Numbers, Joshua (Moses' military leader) led the second generation of Israelites to one military victory after another as they began to move their way north toward the Promised Land. Hence, Moses with the help of Joshua was able to position the Israelites to the east of the Promised Land. They were armed and ready for the invasion.

---

[44] Lev 19:18.

[45] While the Israelites received most of their laws in Exodus and Leviticus, they also received a few extra laws in the book of Numbers including instructions concerning the process of purification via the ashes of a red heifer (Num 19), the instructions for taking and fulfilling a Nazarite vow (Num 6), laws of inheritance (Num 27), and instructions for addressing a jealous husband (Num 5:11ff.).

However, Moses was not allowed to lead them into the Promised Land. How could that be? After leading the Israelites for forty years, Moses was prohibited by God from entering into the Promised Land, because during the journey in the wilderness, Moses had disobeyed God. As was mentioned above, the wilderness where the Israelites wandered had very little water, so in order for them to have water, Moses had to perform the miracle of bringing forth water out of rock. On one such occasion, Moses was directed by God to bring forth water by speaking to the rock. However, Moses disobeyed and struck the rock instead. While God upheld Moses' role by bringing forth water once Moses struck the rock, privately God spoke to Moses and informed him that Moses would not be allowed to enter into the Promised Land. He would die on its border.

Moses' tremendous disappointment in being penalized in this way is reflected in the opening chapters of **Deuteronomy**, the fifth and last book of the Pentateuch. In this book, Moses gave his final speech to the Israelites before his death, and in so doing, he covered a variety of topics. One topic was his frustration with the Israelites and his warning to them that they would face dire consequences if they broke the covenant which they had with God. If Moses would not be allowed to enter the Promised Land due to his disobedience, then the Israelites needed to be aware that they would not be allowed to stay in the Promised Land if they disobeyed God.

Yet, in spite of all of Moses' frustration, in other portions of his speech Moses spoke very eloquently about God and God's love for the Israelites. Also Moses encouraged his people to love God in return. One of the most frequently cited passages in the Bible is within this context. Called the *"Shema"* by the Jewish people because the first word in the passage is *shema* in Hebrew (which means "hear"), this passage was quoted by Jesus in the New Testament as being the most important commandment in the Bible. It is as follows:

> Hear, O Israel: The LORD is our God, the LORD alone. You shall love the LORD your God with all your heart, and with all your soul, and with all your might. Keep these words that I am

commanding you today in your heart. Recite them to your children and talk about them when you are at home and when you are away, when you lie down and when you rise. Bind them as a sign on your hand, fix them as an emblem on your forehead, and write them on the doorposts of your house and on your gates.[46]

As Moses continued through his speech, he commented on the need for the Israelites to obey God by keeping the commandments, avoiding false prophets, and appointing righteous kings from among themselves. After concluding his speech, Moses ordained his military leader Joshua as the next leader of the Israelites, praised God with a special song, exhorted the Israelites to be observant of the law, and uttered a blessing over the Israelites. The book of Deuteronomy then concludes with a eulogy for Moses:

Never since has there arisen a prophet in Israel like Moses, whom the LORD knew face to face. He was unequaled for all the signs and wonders that the Lord sent him to perform in the land of Egypt, against Pharaoh and all his servants and his entire land, and for all the mighty deeds and all the terrifying displays of power that Moses performed in the sight of all Israel.[47]

Concluding Comments on the Pentateuch

With these words, the Pentateuch ends, but the story of Israel is just beginning. According to the books of the Pentateuch, God chose a people who were to be God's representatives on the earth. They were to be a light to the nations, encouraging them to leave false idols behind and to embrace the one true God. However, the Israelites had a difficult time accomplishing this mission. In the next chapter, key events of the struggles and victories of the Israelites as they invaded, settled, and

---

[46] Deut 6:4-9.
[47] Deut 34:10-12.

eventually lost the Promised Land are given as they are reflected in the Historical Books, the next major section of the Old Testament.

Chapter Four
The Historical Books

AS was noted in "Chapter Two", in the original canon of the Old Testament the books following the Pentateuch were called the "Prophets". While the last fifteen books of this twenty-one book section in the Jewish canon are primarily about the utterances of prophets (who maintained they were able to receive and communicate the very words of God to Israel), the first six books in the Prophets detail the history of the rise and fall of the nation of Israel.

When the Christians reordered the books in their canon, they placed these first six historical books in a separate section and added several books from the Writings that also presented portions of the history of Israel. As was noted in "Chapter Two", the Christian world is not in agreement about what books should be in the "Historical Books" section, as the Catholics add more to this section than the Protestants do. The Protestant canon, which is the focus of this textbook, has the following books in the Historical Books section:

Joshua	2 Kings
Judges	1 Chronicles
Ruth	2 Chronicles
1 Samuel	Ezra
2 Samuel	Nehemiah
1 Kings	Esther

The order of the canonization of these books reflects the time in which the books were written. Joshua, Judges, 1-2 Samuel, and 1-2 Kings were mostly written pre-exile (i.e., before the Babylonians destroyed Jerusalem in 587 BCE) while the other books (Ruth, 1-2 Chronicles, Ezra, Nehemiah, and Esther) were mostly written post exile (i.e., after the Persians allowed the Jews to return to Israel approximately 538

BCE). Obviously the difference concerning the date of these books is a reflection of who wrote them and when they were written.

Authorship of the Historical Books

The first six books in the Historical Books section are often referred to collectively by critical scholars as "Deuteronomistic history", because they believe these books echo the mindset reflected in the book of Deuteronomy. Based on their reading of Joshua through 2 Kings, some scholars believe an editor, working after the fall of Jerusalem, utilized documents written earlier to compose a history of Israel demonstrating the periods of obedience and disobedience according to the criteria in the book of Deuteronomy. Referring to this as "Deuteronomistic" editing, these scholars contend Joshua through 2 Kings are a theological history of ancient Israel, promoting Jewish obedience to the Law of Moses along with indicating what occurred in the history of Israel.

Concerning the six books from the Writings that were also placed into the Historical Books section, critical scholars contend that Ruth and Esther are fictional accounts of Jewish heroines written to inspire Jewish obedience during the long years of oppression suffered by the Jews. Concerning Ezra-Nehemiah and 1-2 Chronicles, critical scholars believe these four books were written by a scribe these scholars refer to as the Chronicler, who wrote approximately 300 BCE. The Chronicler was attempting to inspire the Jews still living in exile to return to Judah and resettle the land. Concerning the historical reliability of the Historical Books, critical scholars are very skeptical, contending that many of the events referred to in these books never occurred.

The view of conservative scholars is distinct from the view of critical scholars. Concerning the first six books in the Historical Books, conservative scholars contend: a) Joshua was written by Joshua with the help of a scribe approximately 1370 BCE; b) Judges was written by Samuel, the last of the judges, approximately 1050 BCE; c) 1-2 Samuel were written by an inspired Judean prophet approximately 920 BCE; and d) 1-2 Kings, based on other written documents (most notably the Acts of Solomon, and the Annuls of the Kings of Israel and Judah), were completed by the prophet Jeremiah approximately 550 BCE.

Concerning the remaining six books, these scholars contend: a) Ruth was written by a scribe in the court of King David approximately 970 BCE; b) 1-2 Chronicles and Ezra were written by Ezra, a scribe and son of a priest, approximately 440 BCE; c) Nehemiah was written by Nehemiah, a cupbearer to the king of Persia, who returned to rebuild the walls of Jerusalem approximately 450 BCE; and d) Esther was written by Esther's relative, Mordecai, approximately 460 BCE. Concerning the overall view of the historical reliability of the Historical Books, conservative scholars contend the events referred to in these books actually happened and that they were recorded close to the time they occurred.

Literary Forms in the Historical Books

As it was noted in the previous chapter, the books in the Pentateuch were written utilizing several literary forms including genealogy lists, poetic texts, legal texts, and historical narratives. Similarly, the Historical Books also utilize several literary forms that are in the Pentateuch. For example, the vast majority of passages in the Historical Books are historical narratives. These passages can be analyzed in terms of setting, characters, plot, and point of view. Also, there are several poetic passages, including David's lament over the death of Saul and Jonathan in the opening section of 2 Samuel. There are also a few prophetic passages written in poetic form, including God's promise to David concerning the everlasting nature of his dynasty. Hence, what was presented in the last chapter concerning the analysis of narratives and poetry can be applied to the books in this section.

Content of the Historical Books

The Historical Books pick up the story of ancient Israel where the Pentateuch leaves off. As was noted in "Chapter Three", the book of Deuteronomy closes with a reference to the death of Moses and the appointment of Joshua as the new leader over the Israelites. At that point in time, the Israelites were camped on the east side of the Jordan River waiting for the command to enter into the land of Canaan, the Promised Land. The first book in the Historical Books, the book of **Joshua**, indicates that Joshua received supernatural encouragement to invade Canaan. As Joshua and the people, led by the priests holding the Ark of the Covenant, began to cross the Jordan, the waters of the Jordan parted, allowing them to cross on dry ground, in a similar fashion to how the Israelites crossed the Red Sea under the leadership of Moses. Upon entering into Canaan, Joshua had the Israelites circumcise all of the males, set up a memorial marking the crossing of the Jordan, collect food from the land (no more manna!), and prepare for battle.

The first city the Israelites planned on invading was Jericho. Only a few miles west of the Jordan, Jericho was a walled city in which a woman named Rahab lived. In preparation for the invasion of the land, Joshua had sent two spies to Jericho, and when it was discovered by the authorities in Jericho that two spies were in their land, Rahab hid the two spies and made a deal with them. When they conquered the city of Jericho, they would preserve her life and the lives of her family in return for Rahab's protection. They agreed. The walls of Jericho fell supernaturally once the Israelites marched around the walls for seven days blowing their trumpets, and then the Israelites killed all of the people of the city of Jericho, except Rahab and her family.

After conquering Jericho, Joshua led a military campaign through the center of Canaan, destroying the small city states that existed there. Then he attacked the southern part of Canaan, before turning his attention to the north. After conquering most of the land of Canaan, Joshua ordered the settlement of the land, and it was divided among the twelve tribes. The settlement of the land was the fulfillment of a promise that God made to Abraham, that his descendents would possess the land of Canaan, the Promised Land.

However, after Joshua died, the Israelites struggled for many years with issues of leadership. While the priests were given the task of performing the sacrifices and elders had been appointed during the time of Moses to determine civil cases, there was a political vacuum when Joshua passed from the scene. The internal turmoil in the nation of Israel created problems for the nation externally as foreign powers continually invaded Israel, often subduing it for a lengthy periods of time.

In response to this dire situation, according to the book of **Judges**, God appointed charismatic military leaders to save the people from their enemies. Between approximately 1360 and 1040 BCE, leaders known as "judges" would arise, deliver the Israelites from oppression, and bring peace to the land for a generation. Yet, the peace would not last, and so the land ended up in trouble multiple times for several hundred years. The most significant judges of this time period were Gideon, Deborah, and Samson. Of these three, Samson was the most famous. Born to an elderly couple that had no other children, Samson was told from an early age that he was a special child, a Nazarite,[1] who would deliver his  people from the oppression of the Philistines. In order for Samson to accomplish his task, he was given great strength from God, so much so that Samson was able to kill a lion with his bare hands and kill hundreds of Philistines with the most basic weapons. However, Samson did not

---

[1] Israelites could take a special vow in which they would abstain from drinking alcohol, touching a corpse, and cutting their hair for a period of one to three months. At the end of that time, they would offer a sacrifice commemorating their completion of their vow. In Samson's case, however, the Nazarite vow was not voluntarily taken nor was it only for a brief period of time. He was a Nazarite from birth, and it appears that he resented it.

want to play the role of a deliverer, but rather, he was attracted to Philistine women, including Delilah who ultimately betrayed Samson and delivered him to the Philistines, who gouged out his eyes and made him into a slave. While Samson did avenge the loss of his eyes by killing many Philistines at the end of his life, Samson did not set a good example of someone who followed the law of Moses.

Samson's lack of covenant observance was a continual problem during the time of the judges, and eventually the system broke apart as the tribes began to fight each other. The people of Israel suffered greatly during this time, and in some cases they actually left Israel to find food and security in another country. For example, the book of **Ruth** tells the story of a family with a father, a mother, and two sons who went to the land of Moab looking for food. While they did settle there for several years and the two sons married Moabite women, tragedy followed them there. The father died as did the two sons, leaving three widows to fend for themselves. Eventually two of the ladies (Naomi, an Israelite, and Ruth, a Moabitess) traveled to Israel, and God helped them to rebuild their lives by bringing a good man into their lives, a man named Boaz who eventually married Ruth. From the union of Boaz and Ruth came Obed, the father of Jesse, who was the father of David, the second King of Israel.

The story of Ruth is a good example of God's provision during Israel's national crises. Not only was God interested in the struggles of individuals and families, but according to the book of Judges, God was interested in the welfare of Israel. Each time Israel would become oppressed and then call out to God for help, God would appoint another judge to lead them out of trouble. This cycle lasted until the time of Samuel.

Before Samuel was born, his mother Hannah prayed to God to give her a child, and in return, she promised to give the child to the priest so that the child would be raised in the Tabernacle. According to the book of **1 Samuel**, Samuel was a unique child who was able to hear God's voice at a very young age. Once Samuel became an adult, he was able to lead Israel into a time of covenant renewal and deliverance from the Philistines. However, as successful as Samuel was as a judge (as well as a priest and a prophet), his leadership did not convince the elders of Israel that the system of leadership under the judges was worth continuing. Rather, the elders wanted a more stable system of leadership. They wanted a king like the other nations.

Given that this was the standard model at the time, the Israelites might have chosen this direction earlier. Perhaps one of the reasons they hesitated was due to the perspective that God alone was their king and that they were to be a "nation of priests, a holy nation"[2] in which everyone was equal and lived according to the standards of the Law of Moses and not the whims of an all powerful monarch. However, as attractive as the vision of a theocracy (i.e., God alone is king) might have been to the Israelites, they were not able to embrace their collective responsibility and decided instead to appoint a human king over themselves.

While at first hesitant to do so, Samuel (after praying to God) agreed to appoint them a king. The first king of Israel was Saul. The son of a farmer of the tribe of Benjamin, Saul was a tall handsome man who was not pleased that he had been chosen for this honorable yet difficult task. Even though he was anointed by Samuel and divinely selected to be the first king of Israel, he refused to step into that role until the day came when his people were being threatened by a foreign nation. Seeing the threat to his people and knowing that he had to take action, Saul gathered an army around him and proceeded to drive out the enemy. In spite of his initial reluctance, Saul was a successful military leader, and he was able to stabilize the boundaries of Israel.

Unfortunately, Saul did not get along very well with Samuel. Eventually the relationship between them deteriorated to the point that Samuel no longer supported Saul's leadership, leading Samuel to look for another Israelite to anoint as the next king of Israel. Samuel chose David, a young shepherd boy who played the harp and sang praises to

---

[2] Exod 19:6.

God, many of which are now contained in the book of Psalms (see discussion in "Chapter Five").

Since David was anointed king of Israel before Saul died, it is not surprising that Saul grew to hate David and even tried to kill him on a number of occasions. However, the relationship between Saul and David did not start out this way. Rather, David cared for Saul. Although David was just a young shepherd when he first met Saul, David was helpful to Saul on two levels. First, David was able, through his music, to comfort Saul who had a hard time falling asleep. Second, while only an adolescent and lacking military expertise, David was a fearless warrior for Saul, to such an extent that David killed a mighty Philistine named Goliath of whom the rest of the Israelites were afraid. Because David was so successful, Saul gave David one of Saul's daughters (Mical) to be David's bride. However, the relationship between David and Saul turned for the worst after David became more successful as a warrior than Saul. As a result, Saul became jealous of David and chased him for several years, as he attempted to capture and kill David.

According to the closing chapters of 1 Samuel, Saul eventually died in battle fighting the Philistines. The history of Israel continues with the book of **2 Samuel** which mostly focuses on the kingship of David. After Saul died, David was quickly appointed the king of the southern portion of Israel known as Judah, but the tribes of the north preferred one of Saul's sons as their king. This division lasted for seven years, and during this period there were a number of battles between the north and the south. However, some of the military leaders in the north eventually decided that they wanted David as the king over all of Israel, so they killed Saul's son, and David became the king over all of the land for 33 years.

Initially David's reign was tremendously successful. He more than doubled the size of Israel, as he drove back the enemies of Israel and conquered neighboring countries to the east and the north. Moreover, he conquered an important city within Israel that previous leaders had not been able to conquer. It was David who conquered Jerusalem and made it the capital of Israel. Furthermore, David brought the Ark of the Covenant into Jerusalem, thereby centering both the religious and the political life  of Israel in one place. Not only was David successful militarily, but he was a merciful and wise king who invited another of Saul's sons (who was crippled) to eat at the king's table, one of the highest honors that a king could give to someone. David was so successful and in tune with God's guidance that God promised David that one of David's descendants would always be on the throne in Jerusalem. This promise is known as the Davidic Covenant, which became the foundation for Messianic hopes when the Jews were oppressed by foreign powers hundreds of years after David's death.

Tragically, David's successes did not prevent him from making a flawed decision which would have far reaching consequences. One day while his army was out fighting an enemy, David was on the roof of his palace, looking out over Jerusalem. He saw a married woman bathing on the rooftop of her home, and he had her brought to him. Her husband was not at home, but he was fighting in David's army. David and the woman named Bathsheba had relations that night, and then he sent her home. Later, she sent a message to David indicating that she had became pregnant. The child was David's.

Upon hearing this news, David became afraid, because according to the Law of Moses, if a man and a woman commit adultery, both of them were to be put to death. So David had Bathsheba's husband Uriah brought back from battle, in the hope that Uriah would spend time with his wife. Thus it would appear that Bathsheba's pregnancy was due to her being with her husband. Perhaps suspecting that something was wrong, Uriah refused to sleep with his wife, so David sent Uriah back to battle and arranged for Uriah to meet his death on the frontlines. After Uriah was dead and Bathsheba mourned her husband for a time, David married Bathsheba.

It looked like David was going to get away with adultery and murder. However, according to the second half of the book of 2 Samuel, David was confronted by a prophet named Nathan who knew of David's sin. Nathan told David that tragedy would be in David's family from that time onward. The prophet's words proved true. David and Bathsheba's first child died shortly after being born, and several of David's other children had serious issues.

For example, one of David's sons raped one of David's daughters. Then another son named Absalom took matters into his own hands and killed the brother who had committed the rape. While David did not seek to kill Absalom, he drove him out of the kingdom for a time. When David finally allowed Absalom back, Absalom was bitter and angry with his father to such an extent that he began to use his influence to gain a following among the Israelites. Once his popularity reached an elevated level, Absalom led a revolt against David, driving him out of Jerusalem for a time. Eventually David's army was able to recapture Jerusalem and squelch the rebellion, but in the process of doing so, Absalom was killed. The rest of 2 Samuel presents David's sorrow at the death of his son and how he became increasingly isolated from the people.

According to the opening of **1 Kings**, David's downhill slide became more noticeable as he became older, and one of his sons named Adonijah decided to insert himself as king without his father's approval. Upon finding this out, Bathsheba went to David and convinced him to name Solomon, her second son by David, as the next king of Israel.

Once Solomon was named king, he moved to destroy his enemies as well as those individuals who had made David's life difficult. After cleansing his kingdom from internal enemies by means of an assassin named Benaiah, Solomon began to make military and political alliances with neighboring countries. Like his father, he was tremendously successful in the early years of his reign, not because he was a great warrior like David, but because he was a man of great wisdom who was able to build up the kingdom peacefully. Solomon was a scholar who wrote a number of proverbs as well as studied plant life. He was so successful according to 1 Kings that God decided to allow Solomon to build a Temple. The Temple replaced the Tabernacle, and the Ark of the Covenant was brought into the Temple.

The Temple

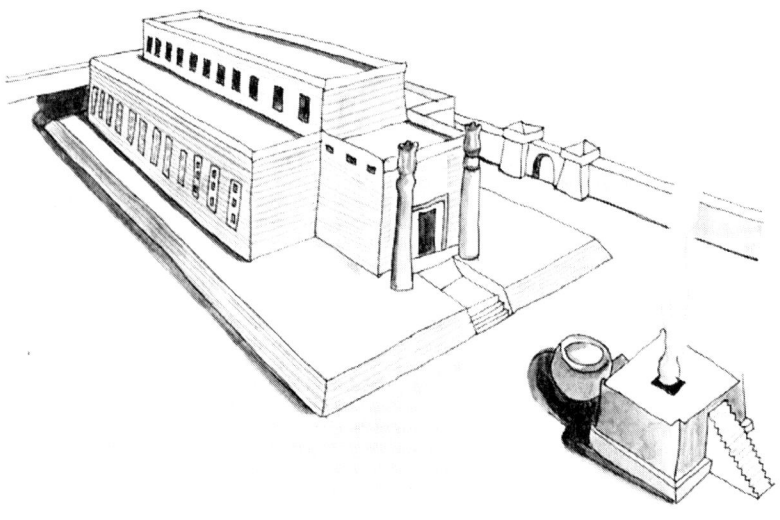

Yet, in spite of all of his success, Solomon eventually found himself at odds with God. As a part of his military alliances with neighboring countries, Solomon married foreign wives who worshipped other gods. As Solomon grew older, apparently he became interested in those other gods and began to worship them. Because of Solomon's disobedience, God sent a prophet to anoint a future king over the northern half of Israel and to speak words of judgment against the southern half of Israel, later known as Judah. The prophecy that was spoken indicated that after Solomon died the nation of Israel would be split into two, and that is what happened.

When Solomon's son Rehoboam became king of Israel, he was approached by elders from the northern tribes who warned Rehoboam that he would be facing civil war if he did not decrease the heavy taxes that his father had enacted in prior years. Rehoboam refused this request, believing that if he gave into the request that it would show weakness. According to 1 Kings, after Rehoboam made his decision, ten tribes located in the northern half of Israel separated themselves and formed another nation with their own king who was named Jeroboam. The nation in the north kept the name Israel, and the kingdom in the south used the name of one of the twelve tribes for the name of its nation. It was known as Judah.

The rest of 1 King and most of **2 Kings** describes what occurred in the history of Israel and the history of Judah. The history of the northern kingdom Israel lasted two hundred chaotic years. Lacking the Davidic dynasty for political stability and access to the Temple for religious stability, the northern kingdom had very few peaceful years during its existence. The kings were often corrupt, and therefore, they would be replaced violently by usurpers to the throne. Each time a king was overthrown, his family would also be killed, so that none of his sons could return to reclaim the throne. A list of the kings of Israel, their approximate years of reigning, and the names of prophets who were active during the kings' reigns are given below:

Kings of Israel

King	Length of Reign	Prophet[3]
Jeroboam I	22 years	
Nadab	2 years	
Baasha	24 years	
Elah	2 years	
Zimri	7 days	
Tibni	5 years	
Omri	12 years	
Ahab	22 years	Elijah
Ahaziah	2 years	
Joram	12 years	
Jehu	28 years	Elisha
Jehoahaz	17 years	
Jehoash	16 years	
Jeroboam II	41 years	Amos, Hosea
Zechariah	6 months	
Shallum	1 month	
Menahem	10 years	
Pekahiah	2 years	
Pekah	20 years	
Hoshea	9 years	Micah

Because the northern kingdom was so chaotic and without long term hope, only a few prophets even attempted to correct the situation. A striking example is the prophet Elijah. According to 1 Kings 18, Elijah had prophesied that the land of Israel would experience a lengthy drought, because the king and queen of Israel were worshippers of the false god known as Baal. In an attempt to demonstrate that his God was the only true God, Elijah challenged the prophets of Baal to a duel. Each side built an altar and then called on their respective gods to bring fire down from heaven, thereby consuming the sacrifice on the altar. The prophets of Baal went first, but in spite of their fervent prayers and

---

[3] The lists of the kings of Israel and Judah and their respective years of reigning are based on reconstruction in *The Bible Visual Resource Book* (Ventura, California: Regal Books, 1989), page 71.

cutting of their flesh,[4] their god did not respond. Then Elijah prayed. The result was overwhelming to the Israelites who were there:

> At the time of the offering of the oblation, the prophet Elijah came near and said, "O LORD, God of Abraham, Isaac, and Israel, let it be known this day that you are God in Israel, that I am your servant, and that I have done all these things at your bidding. Answer me, O LORD, answer me, so that this people may know that you, O LORD, are God, and that you have turned their hearts back." Then the fire of the LORD fell and consumed the burnt offering, the wood, the stones, and the dust, and even licked up the water that was in the trench. When all of the people saw it, they fell on their faces and said, "The LORD indeed is God; the LORD indeed is God."[5]

However, the Israelites did not stay convinced that there was only one God. They continued to drift back into idolatry. Except for the reign of a couple of somewhat obedient kings who brought a bit of stability, the northern kingdom limped along until it was eventually destroyed by Assyria in 722 BCE.

In the south, the kingdom of Judah fared much better. With a stable dynastic monarchy in place based on the Davidic covenant and with a centralized place of worship (the Temple in Jerusalem), the kings of Judah had much more to build upon, and they also benefited from the work of a number of prophets who corrected them when they became disobedient to the covenant. A list of the kings of Judah, their approximate years of reigning, and the names of prophets who were active during the kings' reigns are given below:

---

[4] Some ancient peoples believed that they could influence the deities by shedding blood, either through sacrifice or through cutting their flesh, so that their blood would flow.
[5] 1 Kgs 18:36-39.

Kings of Judah

King	Length of Reign	Prophet
Rehoboam	17 years	
Abijah	3 years	
Asa	41 years	
Jehoshaphat	25 years	
Jehoram	8 years	
Ahaziah	1 years	
Athaliah	7 years	
Joash	40 years	Joel
Amaziah	29 years	
Azariah	52 years	Jonah
Jotham	16 years	
Ahaz	16 years	
Hezekiah	29 years	Isaiah
Manasseh	55 years	
Amon	2 years	
Josiah	31 years	Zephaniah
Jehoahaz	3 months	Habakkuk
Jehoiakim	11 years	Jeremiah
Jehoiachin	3 months	
Zedekiah	11 years	Ezekiel

Given this political and religious foundation, several of the kings of Judah were very successful, having lengthy reigns as they oversaw times of prosperity and peace. For example, King Hezekiah, following the leading of Isaiah the prophet, was a great king who saw God miraculously deliver Judah from the Assyrians who wanted to destroy Jerusalem. Another king who attempted to reform Judah was King Josiah, who tore down shrines dedicated to the worship of idols and dedicated his nation to the obedience of the Torah. Nevertheless, more of the kings were disobedient to the covenant than obedient, and eventually Judah was destroyed by the Babylonians in 587 BCE which is described at the end of 2 Kings.

Up to this point in the discussion of the Historical Books, it has been demonstrated that the story about the history of Israel progresses in a linear fashion from the end of the Pentateuch through the first seven books of the Historical Books. However, the eighth and ninth books of the Historical Books disrupt the chronology. Instead of continuing with the history of Israel after the destruction of Judah, the books of **1-2 Chronicles** actually repeat significant portions of the history of Israel that were already present in other books in the Historical Books. For example, 1 Chronicles covers much of the same time period as 2 Samuel (i.e., the events of David's kingship) while 2 Chronicles covers aspects of the history of Israel that are covered in 1-2 Kings. Given that much of what is in 1-2 Chronicles has already been covered in previous books, why were these books even written?

The answer perhaps can be found in the perspective from which these two books are told. Unlike the stories about David and Solomon in the previous books, the stories about these two kings as told in 1-2 Chronicles are decidedly more positive. For example, in 1 Chronicles there is no mention of David's decisions to commit adultery and then murder to cover up his adultery. Similarly in 2 Chronicles, there is no reference to Solomon's multiple wives and how Solomon became an idol worshipper later in his life. While scholars are not in agreement concerning why the writer of Chronicles chose to write Israelite history from a more positive perspective, it appears that the writer of Chronicles might have been motivated by a desire to promote the Davidic dynasty.

Writing at a time when the Jews were under Persian rule, the Chronicler seemed to be making the case that Israel would be in a much better place if it were ruled by a Jew in the line of David instead of a foreign king. At a first glance, this seems like such an obvious desire (i.e., for a people group to want their own king) that it seems hardly worth stating. However, given the existence of the idealistic presentation of David and Solomon in Chronicles and the much harsher view in Samuel and Kings, it is possible that the Jewish community may not have been in agreement about the need for a Davidic king. After all, the books of Samuel and Kings paint a very unfavorable picture of the Davidic dynasty. It failed to uphold obedience to the Torah, and it failed to stop the destruction of Jerusalem and the Temple. Therefore, in response to those who might have been asking for a Davidic king, there might have been those in the Jewish community who felt like a Davidic king would not make their lives better, because even the two greatest kings in Israel's history (i.e., David and Solomon) failed to keep the covenant. Perhaps it is into this context that the Chronicler felt the need to make his case that in spite of the shortcomings of the Davidic dynasty, Israel was in a much better position with their own king than with a foreign king.

The issue about the need for a Jewish king on the throne in Jerusalem would have become all the more profound when the Temple and the city of Jerusalem were rebuilt in the late 6th and early 5th centuries BCE. According to the book of **Ezra**, after Cyrus the Persian king took control of the Ancient Near East, he allowed the Jews to return to rebuild their capital city.[6] The first step in rebuilding the city was the rebuilding of the Temple. Destroyed by the Babylonians around 587 BCE, the Temple had been the focus of Jewish religion for over 300 years. However, the few Jews who decided to return to Judah and rebuild the Temple faced some significant obstacles. There were forces in Judah that did not want the Temple to be rebuilt, and they caused further delay of the rebuilding for another 20 years.

At that time, two prophets named Haggai and Zechariah arose among the Jews,[7] and these prophets were able to encourage the Jews to complete the rebuilding of the Temple. Approximately 50 years after the Temple was rebuilt around 518 BCE, another Jewish leader named Nehemiah came back to Judah. According to the book of **Nehemiah**, Nehemiah led the Jews in the rebuilding of the walls around the Temple. Like those who had come before him, Nehemiah also faced obstacles and even death threats aimed at stopping the reconstruction of Jerusalem. Yet, Nehemiah pressed forward, completing the rebuilding of the walls and calling for a covenant renewal. According to the books of Ezra and

---

[6] In his time, Cyrus was a very unusual king. Influenced by the teachings of Zoroastrianism (for more information on this religion see http://www.newworldencyclopedia.org/entry/Zoroastrianism), Cyrus held the view that people should be allowed to worship as they saw fit and that they should not be forced to worship foreign deities.

[7] For further discussion of these two prophets, see commentary in "Chapter Six".

Nehemiah, it was Ezra the scribe who was the prominent figure in calling the people to a renewed commitment to the Mosaic covenant. Ezra read the whole Pentateuch aloud, and then he translated the Hebrew text into a language that the Jews understood at the time, which was Aramaic.[8]

While the books of Ezra-Nehemiah describe how a portion of the Jewish people returned to Judah and began to rebuild their nation, the last book in the Historical Books is about Jews who did not come back from exile. The book of **Esther** is a well written story about how Jews in Persia faced severe persecution and yet were able to overcome their enemies. This story opens with the account of a dispute between the king and queen of Persia. According to the narrative, the queen was removed from her position, because she refused to present herself before the king at a party that the king was holding for his closest advisors. After the queen was removed, the king's advisors encouraged him to find the most attractive woman in the empire for his new wife. So the king ordered that all of the beautiful maidens in his land be brought to him. Eventually the king chose a woman named Esther, a young maiden who hid her Jewish identity from the king. The selection of Esther set into motion a string of events which nearly brought about the genocide of the Jews.

After Esther was selected as queen, her relative Mordecai (who had followed her to the city) had a conflict with the king's right hand man named Haman. In response to this confrontation, Haman convinced the king to issue a decree condemning the people group of whom Mordecai was a member. Since Mordecai was Jewish, the decree called for the killing of the Jews to be carried out on a specific date. Once Mordecai found out about the decree, he sent a message to Esther asking her to intervene. The rest of the story of Esther is about how Esther risked her life to save her people. It is one of the most touching and powerful

---

[8] When the Jews were taken into exile to Babylon, they encountered a language similar to their own. Phonetically, their Hebrew language was similar to Aramaic, the language of the Babylonians. Over time the exiles learned the Aramaic language and began to lose their capacity to speak Hebrew. When Cyrus the Persian allowed the Jews to return from exile, they no longer could speak Hebrew fluently. Hence, Ezra had to translated the Hebrew into Aramaic.

stories in the whole Bible, and it gives the historical background for the Jewish holiday of Purim.[9]

Concluding Comments on the Historical Books

As was noted at the end of "Chapter Three", the Pentateuch presented the foundation for the development of the ancient nation of Israel. In the Historical Books, the reader encounters the subsequent history of Israel, from the conquest and settling of the Promised Land, to its destruction at the hands of foreign powers, and finally to the rebuilding of the nation after the exile in Babylon (for a timeline of key events in the Old Testament see Appendix C). In this section of the Bible, God intervenes frequently, attempting to guide the Israelites back to the Mosaic covenant via obedient kings and powerful prophets. However, ultimately the Israelites refused to listen, and therefore, they suffered horrible consequences as their land was invaded and destroyed. At this time, the ten tribes of the northern kingdom known as Israel were mostly assimilated into Assyrian culture. They never returned.

However, many of the people from the southern kingdom of Judah held fast to their beliefs during the time of the exile, and they did not assimilate into Babylonian or Persian culture. Some of them returned and rebuilt the Temple and the city of Jerusalem. Yet, many others stayed in foreign lands. Apparently convinced that it was just as safe in a foreign land as it would be in Judah, many of the Jews (as they became known) chose not to return. Instead of relying upon the rituals connected to the Second Temple, they focused instead on spiritual devotions that could sustain their faith in foreign lands. Some of the texts upon which they relied are found in the next section of the Protestant Bible known as the Poetic Books, which are commented upon in the next chapter.

---

[9] For the Jewish holiday of Purim, Jewish people are encouraged to dress in costumes and have a good time. Along with dressing in costumes, the Jewish people listen to a reading of the book of Esther. As the book is being read aloud in Hebrew, they cheer when Mordecai's name is read and boo when Haman's name is read.

Chapter Five
The Poetic Books

AS was noted in "Chapter Two", in the original canon of the Old Testament several of the books primarily written in poetic form were included in the section called the Writings. However, in the Protestant canon, there is a separate section for these books. Titled simply and appropriately the "Poetic Books", the five books in this section are Job, Psalms, Proverbs, Ecclesiastes, and the Song of Solomon.

Authorship of the Poetic Books

According to conservative scholarship, three of the poetic books were written by the third king of Israel named Solomon. While the last chapters of the book of Proverbs claim to have been written by wise men, Agur, and King Lemuel,[1] the first 22 chapters claim to have been written by Solomon (i.e., "The proverbs of Solomon son of David, King of Israel").[2] Similarly the book of Ecclesiastes, while not as direct, also claims to have been written by Solomon (i.e., "The words of the Teacher, the son of David, king in Jerusalem"),[3] and also the poetic book Song of Songs opens with these words: "The Song of Songs, which is Solomon's".[4] However, critical scholars remain unconvinced by these verses. Contending that the books of Proverbs and Ecclesiastes reflect a long history of editorial work centuries after Solomon's death and that the Song of Songs has linguistic evidence of a time much later than Solomon's reign, critical scholars believe the authorship of these three books is unknown.

Concerning the books of Psalms and Job, there is also a difference of opinion among scholars. Conservative scholars maintain that the

---

[1] Prov 22:17; 30:1; and 31:1 respectively.
[2] Prov 1:1.
[3] Eccl 1:1.
[4] Song 1:1.

statements made in Psalms about the various authors of the Psalms including references to King David (the second king of Israel), Moses, Solomon, and many others are accurate, while critical scholars do not believe these statements can be trusted. Therefore, the critical scholars contend the authorship of the Psalms is unknown. Similarly, critical scholars maintain it is impossible to know who wrote the book of Job, while conservative scholars contend Job himself is the best choice, because Job was the one who experienced what happened in his life.

Literary Forms in the Poetic Books

As was indicated above, the books in this section of the Bible are primarily written in poetic form. While certain aspects of biblical poetry were noted in "Chapter Three", a fuller discussion of poetry, particularly poetry in the Old Testament, is the purpose of this section.

All poetry in the Old Testament has two key aspects. One aspect is called parallelism, and the other involves figures of speech. **Parallelism** is the word used to describe how lines in a verse are related to each other. They are parallel to each other, either building upon each other or are in contrast to each other. Scholars have observed four main types of parallelism.[5] They are as follows:

Synonymous Parallelism: When two or more lines of poetry basically state the same thing using different words, then they are classified as being synonymous. An example of synonymous parallelism is found in Psalm 1:2:

But their delight is in the law of the LORD, (*line 1*)
And on his law they meditate day and night. (*line 2*)

As can be seen in this example, both lines describe a righteous person as one who spends numerous hours studying God's law.

---

[5] For example, see Leland Ryken, *How to Read the Bible as Literature* (Grand Rapids, Michigan: Zondervan, 1984), p. 103f.

Synthetic Parallelism: This type involves the second line completing the idea started in the first line. In other words, both lines are needed to express a single idea. An example of this is found in Psalm 103:12:

As far as the east is from the west, (*line 1*)
so far he removes our transgressions from us. (*line 2*)

In this verse, line one presents an incomplete thought which requires the second half of the verse to complete the idea.

Climactic Parallelism: This type involves the repetition of a phrase or word at the beginning of both lines, and then a different ending attached at the end of each line. An example of this type of parallelism is found in Psalm 29:1:

Ascribe to the LORD, O heavenly beings,
Ascribe to the LORD glory and strength.

As can be seen, the opening phrase is repeated at the beginning of both lines. The emphasis created by the repetition might have been utilized in choruses sung in the Temple in ancient Israel.

Antithetic Parallelism: This type involves a contrast between the two lines, usually between the righteous and the wicked or between the wise and the foolish. An example of this parallelism is found in Psalm 1:6:

For the LORD watches over the way of the righteous,
but the way of the wicked will perish.

In this verse, two ways are placed in contrast to each other. The way of the righteous will flourish, because God makes it so, but the way of the wicked will cease.

The second main aspect of poetry in the Old Testament involves **figures of speech**. Figures of speech are words used in a non-literal fashion in order to create mental images and invoke the senses of the reader. There are several figures of speech, including the following:

Metaphor: A metaphor is a word that defines another word or idea via related qualities. For example, the statement "God is my shield" connects "God" to "shield", implying that just as a shield protects a warrior from the weapons of an enemy, God protects His people from harm. Hence, a "shield" is the mental image for God's protection of His people.

Simile: A simile does much of what a metaphor accomplishes, but the relationship between words is not as direct; they are connected by "like" or "as". An example of a simile is the clause "the tongue is like a sharpened razor." While at a first glance it would not appear that a tongue and a steel razor have much in common, further thought would suggest that both of them can inflict damage to another person. A razor can inflict physical damage, and a tongue can inflict emotional damage.

Hyperbole: This figure of speech involves exaggeration for effect. An example would be the statement "all night I flood my bed with my tears." While people certainly can cry for lengthy periods of time, it is highly unlikely that they are able to create a stream of water in their bed by crying. So what is the point of this exaggeration? Hyperbole is used to reflect the intensity of emotion that exists in a situation. While the image being communicated is an exaggeration, the emotion being expressed in the hyperbole is not.

Allusion: An allusion is a reference to an idea outside of the passage. Often the allusion is to another biblical text. For example, in the sentence "by the word of the LORD were the heavens made" there is an allusion to the act of creation in Genesis 1. According to Genesis 1, God spoke all things into existence. When God said "let there be light", then light was created. A reader who is aware of allusions in a text is able to think about the information in that reference and apply it to the passage being read. Allusions save space and time, because in a few words, they connect the reader to lengthy texts and ideas outside of the passage being read.

Personification: This involves giving inanimate objects human characteristics. For example, the statement "all of the trees of the forest will sing for joy" seems to indicate that trees are crooning. Yet, clearly the reader is not supposed to see trees singing like humans (unless it is a

Disney special); rather the idea is that the trees are caught up in the joy of the moment, and their swaying back and forth in the wind is a reflection of that. The enormity of the emotion of a particular situation is so overwhelming that inanimate objects become animated.

Anthropomorphism: Based on two Greek words,[6] this compound term refers to the concept of giving God human characteristics. For example, notice the following phrase from Psalm 8:3: "When I look at your heavens, the work of your fingers, the moon and the stars that you have established." Here the psalmist (most likely King David) describes God as one having "fingers" with which the celestial bodies are set in place. While the biblical evidence strongly indicates that God is not human or physical, God is often described in human terms, because this makes God more accessible to humans mentally.

All poetry in the Old Testament utilize parallelisms and figures of speech, including poetic passages in the narratives noted in "Chapter Three" (i.e., "songs, blessings and curses, and prophetic oracles") and the Poetic Books referred to in this chapter. Moreover, significant portions of prophetic literature also are poetic in style, and thus they use parallelisms and figures of speech as well (see the next chapter for further commentary). Yet, while all of the poetic passages in the Old Testament have these key similarities, there are several subsets of poetry which have distinct qualities.

As was noted above, the Poetic Books consist of a love song (Song of Solomon), three books focused on life issues (Job, Proverbs, Ecclesiastes), and devotional literature (Psalms). Obviously, the **love song** reflects the drama of human love, so along with noticing the parallelisms and figures of speech in this book, readers need to identify the male and female voices evident in the text. Scholars have long noted that the Song of Solomon reads like a play or an opera in which a man courts a woman and she responds by expressing her own desires.

The three Poetic Books that are focused on life issues have been classified as **Wisdom Literature**. In the ANE, the concept of wisdom

---

[6] The word "anthropomorphism" is based on the Greek words *anthropos* (human) and *morphe* (form).

was widely applied and understood. On the one hand, it was connected to having a particular skill.[7] For example, Babylonian and Egyptian sages were skilled in the interpretation of dreams and the practice of magical arts.[8] Moreover, the sages could write and had public speaking ability.[9] On the other hand, wisdom also was understood more simply as good advice for living a successful and happy life, and it was utilized by families for the training of their children in the home and by kings who sought the best advice for leading their nations.

Whether it was wisdom given to a king or wisdom taught to a child, wisdom was built upon life experiences. Like law, wisdom was built on precedence,[10] founded upon evidence that indicates what the results of an action will be. Wisdom was not abstract or theoretical, but proven truth—truth that has been lived within the context of real life situations.[11] Hence, wisdom literature in the Bible is a collection of teachings that guided the ancient Israelites concerning what they needed to do to survive. The Israelites needed to know how to plant crops, conduct war, and avoid the dangers of immoral living.[12] Some of these ideas were

---

[7] Joseph Blenkinsopp, *Wisdom and Law in the Old Testament: The Ordering of Life in Israel and Early Judaism* (Oxford: Oxford University Press, 1995), 5-6.
[8] Ibid., 9.
[9] Ibid., 15.
[10] "Since both proverbial lore and case or common law are based on precedent and draw their authority from the transmitted wisdom of the past, it is hardly surprising that in Israel the sapiential and legal traditions are so closely connected" (ibid., 21).
[11] Of course humans do encounter contrary experiences, and therefore debates do arise about what to do in a given situation as is reflected in the book of Job. As Gerhard Von Rad maintains experiential knowledge is "complex" and "vulnerable" to change, so it is often generalized (*Wisdom in Law*, [Nashville: Abingdon Press, 1972], 3, 4).
[12] As Gerhard Von Rad notes: "no one would be able to live even for a single day without incurring appreciable harm if he could not be guided by wide practical experience" (*Wisdom in Israel*, 3).

developed through their own experiences and others were borrowed from surrounding cultures.[13]

Wisdom taught in the home was the first line of defense in creating a cohesive highly functional society. When parents took the time to communicate to children what does and does not work in life, they gave their children an advantage, helping them to form a foundation for successful living.[14] This is clearly one of the goals of the writer of the opening portion of Proverbs, who traditionally has been identified as King Solomon. In Proverbs, Solomon writes:

> Hear, my child, your father's instruction
>   And do not reject your mother's teaching;
> For they are a fair garland for your head
>   And pendants for your neck.[15]
>
> Then you will understand righteousness and justice
>   And equity, every good path;
> For wisdom will come into your heart
>   And knowledge will be pleasant to your soul;
> Prudence will watch over you,
>   And understanding will guard you,
> It will save you from the way of evil,
>   From those who speak perversely.[16]
>
> My child, do not forget my teaching,
>   But let your heart keep my commandments;
> For length of days and years of life
>   And abundant welfare they will give to you.[17]

---

[13] The ancient Israelites probably borrowed heavily from the surrounding culture, including from Egyptian wisdom in developing their own wisdom teachings (Blenkinsopp, *Wisdom and Law*, 28).
[14] "The basic assumption of the sapiential tradition in the Near East was that wisdom is a quality of life which can be learned" (ibid., 29).
[15] Prov 1:8-9.
[16] Prov 2:9-12.
[17] Prov 3:1-2.

Parents in ancient Israelite society hoped for the best for their children, encouraging them to learn from the experience of the parents, so that they would not fall into the pitfalls that were in their context.[18] Hence, Israelite proverbs transmitted that culture's values and were a basis for justice in the community,[19] not in an judicial sense, but in the sense that they reflected the created order as established by the God of Israel.[20]

In order to encourage children to accept this instruction, they were told of the benefits that would come to them if they followed the pathway of wisdom, including promises of an inner sense of peace,[21] protection from evil,[22] and length of days.[23] The world was understood as being made by a single deity who embedded human life with consequences related to behavior.[24] Hence, while there is also a subset within wisdom literature that contends that God can choose to ignore human merit and through an act of divine will change human reality based on an unknown objective or standard (as is evident in the book of Job),[25] wisdom in ancient Israel was focused mostly on encouraging the

---

[18] James Crenshaw notes that the "family must surely have been the primary locus for early wisdom" ("The Concept of God in Old Testament Wisdom" in *In Search of Wisdom: Essays in Memory of John G. Gammie* [Louisville, Kentucky: Westminster/Knox Press, 1993], 8).

[19] Blenkinsopp, *Wisdom and Law*, 20, 21.

[20] Leo Perdue notes that "God's own justice permeated creation and was the divine force that sustained its life giving structures" and that God "provided individuals with the organs of perceiving and knowing and gave them the capacity to live wisely and righteously" ("Wisdom in the Book of Job" in *In Search of Wisdom*, 75).

[21] Prov 3:24.

[22] Prov 2:16.

[23] Prov 3:16; 9:11.

[24] Concerning this, Blenkinsopp notes that "to be wise is, in a word, to live in conformity with the law of nature" (*Wisdom and Law*, 23). Similarly, Crenshaw states that "the sages viewed God primarily as the guarantor of a strict system of reward and retribution" ("The Concept of God in Old Testament Wisdom" 3).

[25] As Creshaw notes "the conviction that one escapes vulnerability through proper use of the intellect collapses before the exercise of divine freedom" (ibid., 6). In his commentary on Ecclesiastes, Michael Fox maintains that the reality of impending death can also overwhelm any appeal to wisdom ("Wisdom in Qoheleth in *In Search of Wisdom*, 125). However, Von Rad contends that the

Israelites to seek the blessings that naturally flow from a life lived in accordance with God's created order.[26] Moreover, wisdom literature taught that violation of the created order brought about natural consequences, as created by God.

While wise choices are upheld by God's created order, not everyone agrees what those wise choice are in every circumstance. People have different experiences, and sometimes those experiences are hard to interpret. This dilemma is also evident in the three books classified as Wisdom Literature in the Old Testament.

The book of Proverbs presents wisdom as consistent and achievable. Anyone who desires to be wise simply has to listen to their parents' advice and do the right thing. In so doing, this person assures himself or herself a good life. This type of approach to wisdom is called *prudential*, because right and wrong are presented in a black and white manner.

Job, on the other hand, does not present a single consistent perspective on wisdom. Rather, within the context of this account, Job has a *debate* with his friends concerning what is wisdom. While Job believes he has been unjustly punished, his friends maintain that suffering only happens as a consequence of sin. As commented on below, the debate eventually was settled by God, who stated that human understanding is limited and that it is best not to overreach when it comes to knowledge.

The book of Ecclesiastes is somewhat similar to the book of Job in that it has a more pessimistic approach to understanding life; however Ecclesiastes does not present a debate among several but rather the intense ***quest*** of one man who has lost his way. Having pursued what was supposed to satisfy him (including the study of wisdom), the writer has come to the end of his life only to realize that his material wealth, his

---

scribes in Israel were not overwhelmed by the inconsistencies in life, but rather allowed for mysteries in life which reflect the mystery of God, who ultimately has final say in life, not a set of rules, no matter how well developed and considered (*Wisdom in Israel*, 105-109).

[26] Concerning God's involvement in creation and human interaction with that creation, Von Rad states that "Yahweh encountered man in the world always and only in the individual act of experience" (*Wisdom in Israel*, 63).

earthly pleasures, and even his wisdom were not enough. He will die just like a fool or a dog in the street, and there is nothing that he can do to stop that. After lamenting this reality through most of the book, the writer eventually came to the conclusion that there are some good things in life worth appreciating and that the truly wise thing to do is to take the time to enjoy them and to give thanks to God in the process.

While an analysis of Ecclesiastes must take into consideration the reflective contemplation of a man nearing death, an analysis of the **Psalms** requires a different interpretive approach. To begin with, many of the Psalms open with what is called a *superscription*, which can contain a reference to the author of the Psalm, directions for performing music with the Psalm, and the historical context in which the Psalm was written. When a Psalm begins with this information, it provides the reader with clues that aid the interpretation of the Psalm.

Also an interpretation of the Psalms requires recognizing that Psalms occur in four main types:[27]

Praise Psalms: As the name of these Psalms reflects, praise Psalms offer praise of God for something God has done, said, or is in God's character. Praise Psalms encourage readers to rejoice in the good things of life and express appreciation to God for all that He has done in providing those good things. Praise Psalms have three main parts, including the theme (the main idea of the psalm), the development (an explanation of the theme), and the resolution (a summary of the theme).

Lament Psalms: As the title suggests, this type of psalm expresses the pain and disappointment of the psalmist. Most lament Psalms have five main elements, including: a) a cry to God;[28] b) a complaint about what is causing the psalmist pain;[29] c) a request for relief from the pain;[30]

---

[27] Actually, there are a number of classification systems for the Psalms. Some scholars contend there are 10 or more types of Psalms, but many of those types are variations of the basic four listed above.

[28] An example of a cry to God is: "How long, O LORD? Will you forget me forever?" (Ps 13:1).

[29] An example of a complaint is: "How long shall my enemy be exalted over me?" (Ps 13:2).

d) remembrance of better times with God;[31] and e) a vow to praise God.[32] The pattern of the lament Psalms provides the reader with a method for dealing with pain. The early portion of the Psalm helps the reader to release the pain, and the latter part of the Psalm helps the reader to move forward toward a more positive outlook.

Wisdom Psalms: As the title implies, wisdom Psalms present advice for living, encouraging the reader to consider one pathway versus another. In the process of comparing these pathways, wisdom Psalms often contrast the way of the righteous versus the way of the wicked. Also, these Psalms often include the phrase "happy is the one who" or "blessed is the one who", and they connect the phrase to the pathway of the righteous person. Wisdom Psalms are like praise Psalms in that wisdom Psalms have three main parts in their literary structure: theme, development, resolution (see discussion above).

Royal Psalms: While there are not many Psalms in this category, there are several in which a prayer for the king of Israel is uttered. Recognizing the importance of the king for the well being of Israel, writers of royal Psalms seek divine blessings upon the king of Israel. Hence, it is very likely that these Psalms might have been utilized in a coronation ceremony for the king of Israel. However, some of the Psalms in this category go beyond simply asking for a blessing on the king of Israel. This subset of Psalms projects an idealization of the king of Israel to such an extent that the Psalms seem to call for a new kind of king, a Messiah, who would arise and lead Israel to its place of prominence among the nations. Later interpreters within both the Jewish and the Christian communities contended that these Psalms should be understood as prophecies predicting a future great king who would rule the world. In terms of the structure of these Psalms, they have the same three-fold configuration that is found in the Praise and Wisdom Psalms.

---

[30] An example of a request for relief is: "Consider and answer me, O LORD my God!" (Ps 13:3).
[31] An example of a statement of remembrance is: "But I trusted in your steadfast love" (Ps 13:5).
[32] An example of a vow to praise God is: "I will sing to the LORD" (Ps 13:6).

Content of the Poetic Books

As is noted above, the five poetic books in this section reflect a variety of topics. The book of **Job** is primarily about a righteous man named Job who loses everything at the hands of Satan,[33] who maintained that Job would not keep his faith if he lost everything. According to the book of Job, Satan made this accusation about Job to God. In order to disprove Satan's claims, God allowed Satan to hurt Job, but God did not allow Satan to kill Job.

The testing of Job occurred in two stages. The first stage involved Job's loss of his ten children and all of his wealth in one day. While the loss was devastating to Job, he did not curse God. Rather, Job responded by falling to the ground, worshipping God, and saying: "Naked I came from my mother's womb, and naked shall I return there; the LORD gave, and the LORD has taken away; blessed be the name of the LORD".[34] The second stage involved Job's loss of health. He developed horrible open sores all over his body. This painful development  was too much for his wife, who apparently came to believe that Job must be cursed by God. So she told Job to "curse God and die".[35] One assumes that her comment effectively ended that marriage.

After Job lost his health, he protested his losses, wishing that he had never been born. In response to Job's lament, several of Job's friends, (who had gathered around him during his time of suffering) expressed

---

[33] Scholars disagree concerning who the figure of "Satan" might be. Some contend that Satan is an angel appointed by God to test God's followers in order to determine if they are truly faithful. Others contend Satan is a fallen angel who broke away from God in a past age and, as a rebel in God's kingdom, continually seeks to undermine God and to hurt God's followers.
[34] Job 1:21.
[35] Job 2:9.

their disagreement with Job. In their opinion, Job must have offended God and that is why he was suffering. In reaction against this accusation, Job entered into a debate with his friends. They accused him of sinning, and he defended himself. Eventually God weighed into the debate and corrected them all. Instead of explaining what had happened (i.e., Satan had accused Job before God), God simply noted that there are things in the universe that humans cannot understand and that they should be careful in their analysis of any given situation. Job's friends were wrong in that Job's sufferings were not a result of sin. However, Job was also wrong in his defense in that he went too far, speaking about things that he didn't understand. Upon hearing God's words, Job repented, and God restored him.

Just as the book of Job demonstrates that life can be unpredictable, the book of **Psalms** also reflects the highs and lows of life. Consisting of 150 short songs and prayers, the book of Psalms contains many praises of God for the good things that God has done for individuals as well as for the nation of Israel. Notice, for example, the first verse of Psalm 8: "O LORD, our Sovereign, how majestic is your name in all the earth. You have set your glory above the heavens." Yet, there are also a number of other Psalms that reflect pain and sorrow that people have experienced in life. An example of this type of Psalm is Psalm 3: "O LORD, how many are my foes! Many are rising against me; many are saying to me, 'There is no help for you in God.'" Intermingled with the praise and lament Psalms are a few Psalms reflecting prayers for the king (called Royal Psalms) and Psalms contrasting righteous behavior with wicked behavior (called Wisdom Psalms). The literary forms of these four types of Psalms were discussed above.

Unlike the books of Job and Psalms, the book of **Proverbs** has a much more positive outlook on life. According to Proverbs, a successful life can be achieved and suffering can be avoided as long as a person works hard and does what is right. A few examples of this perspective are obvious in the verses given below:

> The LORD does not let the righteous go hungry,
> But he thwarts the craving of the wicked.[36]
>
> A slack hand causes poverty,
> But the hand of the diligent makes rich.[37]
>
> The desire of the righteous ends only in good;
> The expectation of the wicked in wrath.[38]

According to the opening of Proverbs, this book was written primarily to young people in order to encourage them to live wisely and to avoid making costly mistakes morally, financially, or spiritually. There are basic principles embedded into life, and the wise person knows them and abides by them.

In contrast to the positive outlook of Proverbs, the book of **Ecclesiastes** presents a fairly pessimistic view of life. Apparently writing later in his life when things were not going so well, Solomon (according to the conservative view) reflected on how he had wasted much of his time pursuing things which didn't matter. As he looked back on his life, he didn't feel that his material pursuits or even his intellectual pursuits had brought him satisfaction. Rather, he saw the emptiness of much of what he had done with his time, as he stated in Ecclesiastes 2:16-18:

> For there is no enduring remembrance of the wise or the fools, seeing that in the days to come all will have been long forgotten. How can the wise die just like fools? So I hated life, because what is done under the sun was grievous to me; for all is vanity and a chasing after wind. I hated all my toil in which I had toiled under the sun, seeing that I must leave it to those who come after me.

Yet, after having identified the disappointments in his life, Solomon did find satisfaction in the simple pleasures provided by God: "There is

---

[36] Prov 10:3.
[37] Prov 10:4.
[38] Prov 11:23.

nothing better for mortals than to eat and drink, and find enjoyment in their toil. This also, I saw, is from the hand of God."[39]

Unlike the previous poetic books which are primarily about the joys and struggles in living life, the **Song of Solomon** is a love song in which a man and a woman express their love to each other. Probably written as a duet that was to be performed at a royal wedding, the Song of Solomon glorifies sensual love in a manner that some readers of the Bible have found objectionable. For example, some of the imagery utilized in the song is somewhat graphic in terms of depicting aspects of a woman's beauty. Because of this sensuality, certain interpreters don't believe the Song of Solomon should be interpreted through the lens of human love, but rather through the lens of divine love. Contending that the essence of the song is about God's love for his people, these interpreters encourage readers of the song to understand it allegorically. Other scholars disagree. They maintain that the images and ideas in the Song of Solomon are purposefully glorifying the wonder of human love and sensuality.

Concluding Comments on the Poetic Books

Prior to the Poetic Books, the books of the Pentateuch and Historical Books mostly are in chronological order, including the calling of Abraham, the establishment of the nation of Israel, the downfall of Israel, and its eventual rebuilding. However, the Poetic Books cannot be placed in one specific time period. For example, the book of Job seems to reflect a time prior to the establishment of the nation of Israel, while three of the Poetic Books claim to have been written by King Solomon hundreds of years later. Given this range historically, what can be said about these books as a subset within the canon of the Old Testament?

To a large extent, the contents of the five Poetic Books reflect human responses to a variety of situations, as the ancient Israelite writers attempted to comprehend how life works and where God fits into human existence. They had serious theological questions to ask. For example, is God involved in human suffering? Moreover, is God just? While the

---

[39] Eccl 2:24.

Poetic Books' answer to both of these questions is "yes", it is qualified. There are things that humans cannot understand. There are mysteries humans cannot know. As the authors of the lament Psalms demonstrate, sometimes humans need to express their pain and sorrow when life does not make sense. But that does not mean humans should give up. God is still there and is worthy of praise as the Creator. Therefore, humans also need to celebrate when life goes well. While there are horrible experiences in life, there are also wonderful experiences, like enjoying the fruits of your labor, marveling at the love between a man and a woman, holding a cooing baby, and contemplating the wonders of the universe. The key is to look for the goodness in life and contemplate it, and to avoid those temptations that will lead to a life of misery.

Not only do the Poetic Books call for a life of contemplation, but the last section of the Old Testament, known as the Prophetic Books, does as well. However, the Prophetic Books are less reflective on life in general and more reflective on the covenantal consequences that Israel faced when the nation turned its back on God, as is noted in the next chapter.

Chapter Six
The Prophetic Books

THE last section of the Old Testament in the Protestant canon is a collection of books called the Prophetic Books. According to these books, God spoke directly to individuals known as prophets who then shared that message with the rest of the Israelites.

It is important to note that the concept of prophecy was not a unique idea found only in ancient Israelite society. Many societies in the ANE had a similar concept. Ancient cultures readily accepted the belief that certain individuals called prophets experienced revelation from deities, sometimes via a spoken word and other times via spectacular dreams and visions. Moreover, they believed prophets had been called by the deities to communicate divine ideas to human societies. Hence, prophets were intermediaries between humans and deities.[1]

Sometimes prophets were common people who criticized the status quo, challenging the established religious leaders known as priests who often worked closely with and were supported by kings. Hence, the prophets and the priests could be in conflict with each other. For example, the Israelite prophet Amos was very critical of the religious and political leaders in his time.[2] In other instances, the prophets and priests seemed to coexist, and in fact, could be one and the same.[3] For example,

---

[1] David Petersen, "Introduction", *Prophecy in Israel* (Philadelphia: Fortress Press, 1987), 15.

[2] In Amos 7:10-17, Amos was confronted by Amaziah "the priest of Bethel" who falsely accused Amos of being a professional prophet who could be paid to curse an enemy.

[3] Sigmund MoWinckel contends that initially the ancient Israelite prophet was a seer and priest at the same time. It wasn't until later, when Israel encountered Canaanite culture that the office of seer was "absorbed and replaced by Canaanite nabiism" ("Cult and Prophecy" in *Prophecy in Israel*, 87). Max Weber counters this view, stating that priests and prophets were mostly distinct. While the prophets rejected pay and gained their authority via "revelation and

in ancient Israel a number of prophets also had priestly ties, including Samuel, Ezekiel, and Jeremiah.

Given that there is no consistency in this regard and given that scholars do not agree on how to define a prophet,[4] what can be said about prophecy in Israel? In ancient Israel there was a specific pattern related to the calling of a prophet. According to what can be learned from selected passages in the Bible,[5] a person who considered himself to be a prophet needed to experience a divine calling upon his life. The divine calling had four main parts:

Encounter with God: In a moment of inspiration, the person called to be a prophet encountered God supernaturally in a vision, in a dream, or through a quiet voice in his mind. In this encounter, the prophet was overwhelmed by God's presence.

Realization of Unworthiness: After realizing that the experience was indeed a revelation from God, the prophet would enter deep distress as he realized his sinfulness in contrast to the purity of God. The prophet often felt a sense of doom, believing that his encounter with God would destroy him.

Redemption and Promotion: After the prophet contemplated whether or not his encounter with God would lead to his rejection or death, God redeemed him, forgiving him of his sin and then promoting him to the office of a prophet.

Acceptance of the Calling: Upon realizing God's forgiveness and willingness to promote him to the office of a prophet, the prophet then had to choose either to accept the calling of God or to resist it. Some prophets readily accepted God's calling (such as the prophet Isaiah), but others struggled with the calling before deciding to accept it (such as the

---

charisma", the priests received pay and based their authority on being keepers of the sacred tradition ("The Prophet" in *Prophecy in Israel*, 99).

[4] David Petersen notes that there are various interpretations of prophets, including: "priests, charismatics, ecstatics, poets, theologians, and politicians" and that it is unlikely that the scholarly community will ever reach a consensus on how to define a prophet ("Introduction" in *Prophecy in Israel*, 1).

[5] The four parts of the calling of a prophet can be observed in the calling accounts of Moses in Exodus 3 and of Isaiah in Isaiah 6.

prophet Jonah). Once the prophet finally accepted the calling, then the prophet was told by God what to do (the ministry task), whom to go to (the audience), and what to say (the message).[6] Over time, prophetic utterance was edited and written down, forming the prophetic texts that are known today.

Within Israel's prophetic texts, it is obvious that there were two primary concerns. One concern was that Israel needed to be encouraged to stay loyal to the Mosaic covenant. When Israel ignored the logic of wisdom and the requirements of the law, then God, via a prophet, took a more direct line of attack. Consider, for example, the following passage from the book of Isaiah:

> When they say to you, "Consult the mediums and the spiritists who whisper and mutter," should not a people consult their God? Should they consult the dead on behalf of the living? To the law and to the testimony! If they do not speak according to this word, it is because they have no dawn. They will pass through the land hard-pressed and famished, and it will turn out that when they are hungry, they will be enraged and curse their king and their God as they face upward.[7]

If Israel sought its counsel outside of the law, then they could expect catastrophe to come upon them from the hand of God, who could no longer depend on just courts or leaders to bring correction to the people. For example, in the time of Isaiah, the elder and the princes of the people became greedy, as they accumulated wealth at the expense of the poor.[8] While even animals have the basic common sense to appreciate their masters, the Israelites failed to acknowledge their God, and became a people who lacked understanding.[9] Due to these failures, God, speaking through the prophet Isaiah, warned of impending doom that God would

---

[6] Herman Gunkel notes that prophets were first and foremost speakers ("The Prophets as Writers and Poets" in *Prophecy in Israel*, 24).
[7] Isa 8:19-21.
[8] Isa 3:13-15.
[9] Isa 1:3.

bring upon them. God warned that he would raise up an army from the north and that army would devastate the land. Supernatural consequences were enforced by God when natural and legal consequences failed to redirect Israel.

Another primary concern expressed in the prophetic text was that the Israelites needed to be encouraged to accept God's forgiveness after a time of punishment. After Israel experienced suffering often through the oppression of a foreign country, God, via the prophets, would encourage the Israelites to receive comfort from God and reestablish their country, resting on the knowledge that their covenant with God was still intact. A good example of this type of prophecy is found in the book of Isaiah:

> Comfort, O comfort my people, says your God. Speak tenderly to Jerusalem, and cry to her that she has served her term, that her penalty is paid, that she received from the LORD's hand double for her sins.[10]

Written to the Israelites (known as Jews at that time) who had experienced the dominance of the Babylonians, this passage attempted to encourage them to return to the land of Israel and rebuild their country. This movement back and forth between warnings of impending judgment and words of comfort are found throughout the Prophetic Books as is demonstrated below.

Authorship of the Prophetic Books

Given that the prophets experienced God's revelation and then communicated that revelation to the people of Israel, conservative scholars contend that it was the prophets themselves or close associates of the prophets who wrote the Prophetic Books. Hence, from this perspective, the prophet Isaiah wrote the book of Isaiah, the prophet Jonah wrote the book of Jonah, and the prophet Malachi wrote the book of Malachi. Contending that the Prophetic Books accurately present God's actual words to the prophet, conservative scholars maintain that

---

[10] Isa 40:1-2.

information about events that occurred much later than the time of the prophets was given to the prophets by God ahead of time in order to prepare God's people for those future events.

However, critical scholars do not agree with this premise. Critical scholars contend that it is not possible for a human to know about events before they actually happen. They do not believe in supernatural revelation. Therefore, critical scholars contend that much of the content in prophetic books was written years after the prophets were dead. Critical scholars maintain that those facing national crises wanted to encourage the ancient Israelite community to believe that God had not abandoned them. According to these scholars, prophecies like the one in Isaiah chapter 45 (which presents detailed information about how a king of Persia will free the people of Judah and allow them to return to the land of Judah) could not have been written a long time before the event actually occurred. Rather, they contend that an unknown scribe wrote down the so called prophecies after the events occurred and then labeled them as having come from the prophet Isaiah. Clearly conservative and critical scholars have a significant difference of opinion about the authorship of the Prophetic Books.

Literary Forms in Prophetic Texts

While there are a few scattered narratives in certain Prophetic Books, much of the literature in these texts is poetic in form. Therefore, most passages in the prophetic literature can be analyzed like other poetry in terms of the parallelisms and the figures of speech (see "Chapter Five" for commentary). However, the content of the Prophetic Books is quite distinct from other poetry in the Bible.

Classified as a subset of visionary literature by literary critics, **prophetic literature** presents oracles of God in a cyclical fashion. As was noted above, judgments against God's people and promises of restoration of God's people alternate, with very little and often no transition indicating when one begins and the other ends. One of the biggest challenges a reader of prophetic literature faces is that of following the abrupt changes in the text. For this reason, it is important to recognize the style of writing utilized for judgments and promises.

Promises of restoration are presented in a declarative style, as God indicates clear intent to save Israel from dire situations. An example of a promise of restoration is found in Isaiah 1:26-27:

> I will restore your judges as at the first, and your counselors as at the beginning. Afterward you shall be called the city of righteousness, the faithful city. Zion shall be redeemed by justice, and those in her who repent, by righteousness.

The prophetic promises were based on God's loyalty to the covenant that God had made with the Israelites. Hence, the promises are stated in a straight forward style of writing.

While the promises are in the form of declarations of God's intent, the judgment oracles occur in several distinct styles of writing:

Woes: Some of the judgment oracles list the charges that God has against the ancient Israelites, and each charge is preceded by the word "woe" or "alas" which in Hebrew is an interjection (like the phrase "look out"). An example of this is found in Habakkuk 2:6: "Alas for you who heap up what is not your own!"

Judicial: Some of the judgment oracles read as though they were written by a prosecuting attorney making his or her case before a court of law. A good example of this is found in Isaiah 1:2 where God invokes the heavens and earth to hear God's case against the people of Judah: "Hear, O heavens, and listen, O earth; for the LORD has spoken: I reared up children and brought them up, but they rebelled against me."

Explanation: Some of the judgment oracles are explanatory, giving the reasons for God's anger with Judah or Israel and the basis for why God will punish those who violate the Mosaic Covenant.

Along with the recurring cycle of judgment and promise, prophetic literature often presents images that are difficult to understand. Some of the images are simply symbols representing a spiritual or physical reality explained in the text itself. For example, in the book of Jeremiah, Jeremiah saw a vision of a boiling pot. The explanation of this image is given in the very next verse: "Then the LORD said to me: 'Out of the north disaster shall break out on all the inhabitants of the land."[11] The disaster from the north was the Babylonian army coming upon Judah. Other images in prophetic literature refer to heavenly realities. A good example of this is found in Ezekiel 1:4-7:

> As I looked, a stormy wind came out of the north: a great cloud with brightness around it and fire flashing forth continually, and in the middle of the fire, something like gleaming amber. In the middle of it was something like four living creatures. This was their appearance: they were of human form. Each had four faces, and each of them had four wings. Their legs were straight, and the soles of their feet were like the sole of a calf's foot; and they sparkled like burnished bronze.

As can be seen from the above text, it can be difficult to conceptualize what the prophet was seeing. When encountering this type of image, it can be helpful to look at how artists have interpreted them.

Raphael's Painting of Ezekiel's Vision

---

[11] Jer 1:14.

As was mentioned above, prophetic literature is only one subset within the larger category of visionary literature. The other subset is called **apocalyptic literature**. This literary form appears in an incipient form in some of the Prophetic Books, including the books of Isaiah, Ezekiel, and Zephaniah. A more fully developed form of apocalyptic literature is evident in one prophetic book, the book of Daniel (see commentary below).

While built upon and parallel to prophetic literature, apocalyptic literature contains several distinctive features including:

A Hero in the Community of Faith: While prophetic literature is built upon the premise that an imperfect prophet receives revelation from God and records his experience, apocalyptic literature is based on the premise that a blameless faithful hero in the Jewish community has been selected by God to know future events. This hero is not considered to be a prophet.

Supernatural Revelation Communicated through an Angel: While the hero can and does see visions and dreams similar to what the prophets experienced, the hero in apocalyptic literature also is visited by angels who often explain complicated visions to the hero.

The Future is Pre-Determined: In prophetic literature, how events of the future might unfold depends to some extent on the decision made by God's people. Often the prophets placed a choice before the Israelites. If they chose to obey God, the future would be bright and prosperous. They would have a good life. However, if they chose to continue to disobey God, then their future would be dark. They would experience horrible suffering.

In apocalyptic literature, the Jews were confronted with a different scenario. No longer in control of the land of Israel and with many of them living in foreign lands, they had little choice concerning how they would be treated. Hence, they could be very obedient to God and still experience horrible suffering. They were persecuted for their faith.

Apocalyptic literature attempted to encourage the Jews to remain faithful regardless of what they might experience at the hands of others. In fact, in apocalyptic literature such as the book of Daniel, they were told that the oppression by foreign powers was not going to end any time soon. One oppressive nation after another would arise, and there wasn't anything they could do about it.

Hope is Deferred: While in apocalyptic literature people were not given the option of choosing a brighter immediate future, they were encouraged to defer their hope for a better life now for a hope of eternal life with God. This world is not going to get any better. Therefore, it is better to focus on solidifying a relationship with God, who lives beyond the immediacy of this world. Evil will have its day, but it won't last. God lives forever, and so do those who worship God.

The Content of the Prophetic Books

While many of the Prophetic Books focus on the need for Israel to repent of sin before God brings judgment, these books also have distinctive elements. Some of the key distinctive elements in each book are presented below:

Isaiah (written approximately 700 BCE):[12] Biblical scholars usually divide the book of Isaiah into three main sections. The first section (chapters 1-39) focuses on how Judah failed to obey God and therefore would be under Assyrian threat for several years. However, God promised to deliver Judah from Assyria and not to allow Jerusalem to be captured. In part, God was willing to do this because a special child would be born in Judah who would become the king. During his reign, God promised to destroy the Assyrian threat. Many scholars maintain that this child was Hezekiah who later became king of Judah, but other scholars believe that the prophecy refers to a future king who would be the Messiah. For example, conservative Christian scholars contend that this prophecy refers to Jesus, who lived in the first century CE. While the prophecies in Isaiah 1-39 indicated Jerusalem would survive the

---

[12] All dates given in this section are based on the view of conservative scholars who maintain that each prophetic book was written during the life time of the prophet for whom each book was named. Information for the dating of these books according to critical scholarship can be found in the introductions to the Prophetic Books in *The New Oxford Annotated Bible*.

Assyrian threat, ultimately Jerusalem would not escape destruction. This section closes with a warning that the Babylonians will come someday and capture Jerusalem.

Reflecting a period of approximately 150 years after the death of Isaiah, the second section (chapters 40-55) focuses on the aftermath of the Babylonian invasion. The people of Judah had experienced the horror of the capture of Jerusalem, and many of them were taken into exile in Babylon or they fled and became refugees in other nations such as Egypt. In this section of Isaiah, the people of Judah were encouraged to return to Judah and rebuild their land. Their sins had been paid for by their own suffering,[13] and their time of punishment had come to an end.

Reflecting a period of approximately 200 years after the death of Isaiah, the third section (chapters 56-66) focuses on the difficulties the people of Judah faced in rebuilding their nation after returning from exile. One of their problems was that they were few in number. Most of the people of Judah, who became known as the Jews, did not return from foreign lands. Hence, it was difficult for the small number of returning exiles to rebuild the nation of Judah. Another problem they faced in rebuilding the nation was that some of those returning were not worshipping God but were worshipping other deities. In the first section of the book of Isaiah, sinful behavior such as this was punished collectively. The whole nation of Judah paid the price. Yet, in the last section of Isaiah, each individual was encouraged to follow God, because God would bless each one with internal peace if he or she repented. Those who sinned would pay the price for their own sin. There would not be another shared punishment.

Jeremiah (written approximately 575 BCE): Called the weeping prophet, Jeremiah was probably a teenager when he sensed that God wanted him to be a prophet. Born at a time when the nation of Judah was fairly stable, Jeremiah lived through the decline of Judah and its eventual demise at the hands of the Babylonians. He was living in Jerusalem when the Babylonians captured the holy city and watched as his countrymen were slaughtered. Yet, as horrible as that experience must have been for

---

[13] See Isa 40:1ff.

Jeremiah, it was his fore knowledge that Jerusalem was going to fall that caused Jeremiah tremendous agony for many years prior to Babylon's actual attack. Sensing that resistance to the Babylonian threat would be futile and that it would cause the unnecessary deaths of thousands of his countrymen, Jeremiah attempted to warn the king of Judah and the people of Judah against resisting the Babylonians. Tragically, they wouldn't listen. The book of Jeremiah indicates that Jeremiah was rejected, accused of being a false prophet, thrown into prison, and had his earliest written prophecies burned.

Yet, for all of the tragedy in his life, Jeremiah did not lose hope. Along with the horrors that he felt were coming, he also believed God would eventually restore the people of Israel and Judah, enacting with them a new covenant, forgiving them of their sins.

Lamentations (written approximately 575 BCE): This brief book originally was included in the Writings section of the Jewish Bible. However, it was placed after the book of Jeremiah in the Christian Old Testament due to the view that the book was written by Jeremiah. As the title indicates, this book is a lament over the destruction of Jerusalem. While the book of Jeremiah foretold the destruction of Jerusalem, Lamentations was written after the destruction, and it attempted to capture the overwhelming sense of grief that the writer had over this tragic event.

Ezekiel (written approximately 562 BCE): After the Babylonians defeated the Assyrians around 609 BCE and the Egyptians around 605 BCE, they became the dominate power in the Ancient Near East. As such they controlled Judah. In reaction against Babylonian oppression, the Judeans attempted to rebel, but they were unable to drive the Babylonians out of Judah. Rather, Babylonian pressure increased, and they laid siege to Jerusalem in 597 BCE, eventually capturing the city and forcing many of the leaders of Judah into exile. Ezekiel, the son of a priest, was taken into exile into Babylon at that time. After arriving in Babylon, Ezekiel began having supernatural visions in which he saw spectacular heavenly scenes reflecting the presence of God and horrific earthly scenes in which the corruption of the priests of the Temple in Jerusalem was exposed.

In the context of these visions, three main themes emerge. First, Ezekiel indicated to the exiles in Babylon that God's presence was mobile. God was not bound to the Temple in Jerusalem, but God moved freely about. The good news connected to the mobility of God was that God could be found wherever the Jews might find themselves. The bad news was that God would not protect the Temple in Jerusalem from attack by the Babylonians. The Temple would fall. Second, God was aware that not everyone in Jerusalem had committed a sin worthy of death, and therefore, God would place a supernatural mark on the faithful inhabitants of Jerusalem. They would not be allowed to be killed when the Babylonians invaded the city. Third, even though Jerusalem would be destroyed, God would not give up on the Jews. Rather, God would renew the covenant with those Jews who desired a relationship with God. No longer would God punish the nation of Judah due to the sins of its leaders. Instead, each person would be punished or rewarded according to his or her deeds:

> What do you mean by repeating this proverb concerning the land of Israel, 'The parents have eaten sour grapes, and the children's teeth are set on edge'? As I live, says the Lord GOD, this proverb shall no more be used by you in Israel....it is only the person who sins that shall die.[14]

As can be seen in the above passage, according to this prophecy of Ezekiel, God envisioned a time when each Jewish person would be held accountable only for his or her actions and not the actions of a previous generation.

Daniel (written approximately 600 BCE): Like the book of Lamentations, the book of Daniel was originally placed in the Writings. Its placement in the third section of the Jewish canon was due to its literary form (apocalyptic literature, not prophetic) and perhaps due to

---

[14] Ezek 18:2-4.

the possibility that it was written later than the other Prophetic Books. Since the book of Daniel presents detailed information about the rise of the Greek empire and its impact on Israel in the fourth through the second centuries BCE, some scholars maintain this book was not written by Daniel around 600 BCE. Rather, it was written by an unknown Jewish scribe around 150 BCE.

Concerning the overall content of the book of Daniel, it can be divided into two main sections. The first section is a narrative about the life of Daniel and his friends in Babylon. Taken earlier into exile than Ezekiel (see commentary above), Daniel was a faithful believer in God who refused to eat non-kosher food or worship the deities of the Babylonians. Because of his piety and his influence upon king Darius (who took over the Babylonian empire after king Nebuchadnezzar died), certain jealous Babylonian officials accused Daniel of being disloyal to the king. As a result, Daniel was thrown into a den of lions. Yet, Daniel miraculously survived, and his accusers were subsequently put to death by the king.

The second half of the book of Daniel focuses on a series of visions that Daniel saw concerning the future of Israel. According to Daniel chapters 7-12, Daniel saw the rise and fall of the empires of the Babylonians, the Medes, the Persians, and the Greeks.[15] Yet, while the Jews would be oppressed for hundreds of years by one great super power after another, they were not to give up hope. The oppressive kingdoms, represented by horrific animals in the visions in Daniel, would eventually come to an end.

---

[15] While some scholars believe these four kingdoms are referred to in Daniel 7, other scholars contend the four kingdoms referred to in Daniel 7 are Babylon, Persia, Greece, and Rome.

Beasts Representing Oppressive Kingdoms in Daniel 7

Daniel foresaw that God would not abandon the Jews but would eventually grant them an eternal kingdom if they would honor God by being a holy people. This vision of God's desire to bestow upon the holy people an eternal kingdom contains a reference to a coming "son of man". While this term is explained in terms of a collective allusion to God's holy people within the context of Daniel 7,[16] in the New Testament Jesus used the term in reference to his ministry. Hence, some scholars view Daniel 7 as a Messianic prophecy referring to Jesus. However, other scholars note that Jesus utilized the "son of man" reference in order to introduce a new paradigm of spirituality. Those who are truly God's people don't use violence to gain their authority, but rather gain their authority as a gift from God due to their obedience (see further commentary in "Chapter Eight").

---

[16] See Daniel 7:27 which states: "The kingship and dominion and the greatness of the kingdoms under the whole heaven shall be given to the ***people*** of the holy ones of the Most High; their kingdom shall be an everlasting kingdom, and all dominions shall serve and obey them."

Hosea (written approximately 722 BCE): Written during the life time of the great prophet Isaiah in the southern kingdom of Judah, this prophetic book focuses on the northern kingdom of Israel and how Israel failed to be obedient to the Mosaic Covenant.[17] This book is distinct from the other Prophetic Books in that it contains an unusual object lesson. According to the book of Hosea, the prophet Hosea was commanded by God to marry a prostitute, and his marriage to this prostitute would be a reflection of God's relationship to Israel. While God loved Israel and continually attempted to draw closer to Israel, Israel preferred chasing after other lovers (i.e., deities). Therefore, God was going to allow this nation to be destroyed by Assyria. Then the Israelites would wander among the nations for a time before God brought them back.

Joel (written approximately 825 BCE): While this Prophetic Book is not first canonically, many scholars believe it is the first chronologically. Supposedly written during the reign of King Joash of Judah, the book of Joel warned the people of Judah of impending judgment if they continued to follow the idolatry of their errant king. Joel warned them that the "day of the LORD" would come, a day of destruction and horror, unless they repented. However, even if they didn't repent, God would not give up on them, but a day would come when God would greatly bless Judah:

> I will pour out my spirit on all flesh; your sons and daughters shall prophesy, your old men shall dream dreams, and your young men shall see visions. Even on male and female slaves, in those days, I will pour out my spirit.[18]

In the first century CE, the above prophecy was interpreted by the writer of the book of Acts in the New Testament as a reference to the blessing

---

[17] After the death of King Solomon, the nation of Israel split into two, with the northern half keeping the name "Israel" and the southern half using the name "Judah".

[18] Joel 2:28-29.

of the Holy Spirit, a transforming infilling of God's Spirit among the early Christians.

Amos (written approximately 750 BCE): According to the book of Amos, Amos was a farmer who was called by God to warn Israel, Judah, and the surrounding nations that God would punish them for their sins. This book focuses on how religious people can fool themselves into believing that they are righteous by simply performing religious rituals. Amos warns such people that only ethical behavior impresses God, including taking care of the poor, upholding justice, and being economically fair to all people.

Obadiah (written approximately 580 BCE): As the shortest of the Prophetic Books, the book of Obadiah is focused on a single issue. According to Obadiah, the nation of Edom would be destroyed by God, because even though the Edomites were distant relatives of the people of Judah, the Edomites took advantage of Jewish suffering when Babylon invaded Judah. When the people of Judah were fleeing the devastation caused by Babylon, the Edomites attacked the fleeing refugees, robbing them of their meager possessions. Therefore, God was going to send horrible devastation upon Edom. It would cease to exist.

Jonah (written approximately 750 BCE): Presenting one of the most well known stories of the Bible, the book of Jonah gives the account of a prophet named Jonah who was called by God to go to Nineveh, the capital of Assyria (it was located in modern day Iraq), and proclaim a warning to the city in the hope that the Ninevites would repent and avoid God's impending wrath. However, Jonah did not want to go to Nineveh, which was east of Israel. He hated the Assyrians, because they were enemies of the Israelites. So Jonah attempted to run away from God by embarking on a journey by ship on the Mediterranean to the west of Israel.

In response, God sent a great storm upon the sea, causing the superstitious sailors to cast lots and determine who among them had angered the gods.[19] When the lot fell on Jonah, the sailors, after some hesitation, threw Jonah overboard. According to the book of Jonah, God

---

[19] At that time, people believed all natural occurrences were caused by the gods.

then caused a whale to swallow Jonah until Jonah repented and agreed to do God's bidding. After the whale spit Jonah back onto the sea shore, Jonah went to Nineveh and proclaimed the message of God. However, when the Ninevites repented as God expected, Jonah protested God's decision not to punish the Ninevites. In response, God asked Jonah a question, thereby ending the story:

> Should I not be concerned about Nineveh, that great city, in which there are more than a hundred and twenty thousand persons who do not know their right hand from their left, and also many animals?[20]

While many of the Prophetic Books present foreign nations as either God's instruments to punish Israel or as those who will be judged for mistreating Israel, the book of Jonah demonstrates that God's concern was not only with Israel, but also with the other people groups of the earth.

Micah (written approximately 700 BCE): A contemporary of the prophet Isaiah, the prophet Micah warned that the northern kingdom of Israel would fall to Assyria due to its idolatry. However, the southern kingdom of Judah, even though poisoned by Israel's example and threatened by Assyria, would not fall. Rather, Judah would be saved, in part due to the leadership of a great king who would be born in Bethlehem. This king would lead Judah back toward God and reestablish justice in the land, thereby restoring Judah and creating an example of holiness that the other nations could see and emulate. Some scholars believe the king referred to was King Hezekiah during whose reign the Assyrians were driven back supernaturally. However, other scholars maintain that the prophecy is about a future king, a Messiah. The writer of the Gospel of Matthew in the New Testament indicated that he believed this prophecy referred to Jesus.[21]

---

[20] Jonah 4:11.
[21] See Matt 2:5-6.

Nahum (written approximately 650 BCE): Written one hundred years after the book of Jonah, the book of Nahum prophesies the end of the Assyrian empire. Unwilling to acknowledge that its ascent was due to God's intervention and the call to repentance via the ministry of Jonah, the nation of Assyria became arrogant, flaunting its power in front of the nations and contending that no deity could stop the Assyrians from destroying whomever they wished to conquer. Therefore, through the prophet Nahum, God foretold of Assyria's defeat at the hands of the Babylonians forty years before it happened.

Habakkuk (written approximately 630 BCE): 70 years after the time of Isaiah, Habakkuk also foretold of the rise of the Babylonians and the destruction of Judah. Also, like Jeremiah, Habakkuk struggled with this vision. While he agreed that Judah had strayed from God and deserved punishment, Habakkuk couldn't understand how God could use an evil empire like Babylon for God's purposes. In response, God told Habakkuk that God has the right to use the nations as God sees fit. God is sovereign, and those who want to serve God must have faith, particularly when they don't understand what God is doing.

Zephaniah (written approximately 626 BCE): A contemporary of the prophet Jeremiah, Zephaniah wrote his prophecy during the reign of king Josiah of Judah. According to the book of Zephaniah, Judah was in trouble, because the people of Judah had been worshipping idols, and the leaders of Judah had failed. The political leaders were taking advantage of the poor, the prophets were reckless, and the priests were violating the Law of Moses. Therefore, Zephaniah warned them that the Day of the Lord was near; judgment was coming upon them quickly unless they repented. Yet, this prophetic book concludes on a positive note, as God promises to purify the people of Judah and re-gather them after the exile.

Haggai (written approximately 520 BCE): Unlike the previous Prophetic Books, Haggai was written after the exile. The people of Judah had been allowed to return from exile under the reign of King Cyrus the Persian who had defeated the Babylonians. However, while the Jews had been allowed to return in 538 BCE and were also permitted to rebuild the Temple in Jerusalem, they encountered significant resistance and were having a difficult time completing the rebuilding. After receiving visions from God, Haggai attempted to encourage the Jews to complete the rebuilding project by reminding them that while they were living in homes, God's house was desolate. Moreover, if they completed the project, they could expect a tremendous blessing of God upon them, as God provided rain for a bountiful harvest and forced the nations to bring wealth and glory to Israel.

Zechariah (written approximately 520 BCE): A contemporary of Haggai, the prophet Zechariah also wrote about the need to rebuild the Temple, except Zechariah was more specific in his encouragement, and also he presented other topics related to his time. Concerning the rebuilding of the Temple, Zechariah wrote to encourage two Jewish leaders, Joshua (a priest) and Zerubabel (a political leader), to depend on God and lead the completion of the Temple. Concerning other topics, Zechariah indicated that: a) God sent angelic patrols upon the earth which reported back to God; b) the re-gathering of Judah to the Promised Land would bring a blessing to the other nations; c) Israel's future king would be humble; and d) Jerusalem would be protected, because God ultimately was its king. The third topic in this list became significant for certain writers of the New Testament, because they believed Jesus was the humble king who rode into Jerusalem on a donkey.[22]

Malachi (written approximately 475 BCE): The last prophetic book presents visions reflecting a period in Judah's history approximately 40 years after the building of the Second Temple. A Persian governor was ruling in Jerusalem, and the Jews were struggling to maintain their devotion to God. According to the book of Malachi, the Jews were bringing inappropriate sacrifices to the Temple, teaching inaccurate interpretations of the Law of Moses, divorcing their wives for insufficient reasons, and wearying God with their false words. In order to restore right worship and religious practice, the prophet Malachi told them that they needed to repent, discern between good and evil, separate themselves from the wicked who would be destroyed, and remember the teachings in the Law of Moses. Moreover, Malachi prophesied that a

---

[22] See Matt 21:1-11.

messenger was coming to purify the people. This messenger, referred to as Elijah,[23] would restore the Jews, turning them back to God.

In Jewish tradition, this prophecy is retold at the time of Passover. At the end of the Passover meal commemorating the deliverance of the Israelites from slavery in Egypt, a cup of wine is placed on the table, and the front door is opened. Then Elijah is invited to enter the home and declare that the Messiah has come. In Christian tradition, this prophecy is utilized in reference to John the Baptist, who in the New Testament is viewed as the prophet ushering in the time of Jesus, whom Christians believe is the Messiah.

Concluding Comments on the Prophetic Books

While there are seventeen books in this section of the Protestant canon, to a large extent the Prophetic Books focus on two main themes. First, they contain warnings to the community of Israel concerning punishments that will come upon the community if it strays from the Mosaic Covenant. Israel was to be a light to the nations, reflecting the justice and mercy of God. If they failed in this task, then not only wer they in danger of judgment but also the other nations would lose this important example. So there was much at stake. Based on the curses of the covenant God made with Israel via the mediation of Moses, the warnings in the Prophetic Books reminded the Israelites that they were in a binding relationship with a jealous deity who would not tolerate disobedience and disloyalty. Hence, the Israelites were threatened with famine, plagues, and attacks from foreign powers if they pursued worship of other gods.

Second, the Prophetic Books contain promises of God's forgiveness and restoration of the nation of Israel. These promises can be divided into two subsets. One type of promise involved God's willingness to stop the punishments from coming upon Israel if the Israelites ceased their

---

[23] As was noted in "Chapter Four", Elijah was a great prophet who battled the prophets of Baal, and he was able to demonstrate to the Israelites the power of the God that he served.

idolatry and turned back to God. Another type of promise involved God's commitment to restore Israel at a future date even if Israel continued on its pathway of idolatry and had to be punished. This type of promise included God's vow to purify Israel through the suffering caused by the invasion of foreign powers, the destruction of Jerusalem, and the forced exile of many Israelites. After the period of punishment was completed, God promised to bring the Israelites back to the land of Israel.

It is within the prophecies about the restoration of Israel that a reader also will find statements about an idealized future, an age in which the leaders of Israel will truly follow God and promote a society of justice and equality. While some interpreters maintain these prophecies only point to a higher ideal (i.e., a "messianic age"), other interpreters contend these prophecies point to a future great king. The traditional Jewish interpretation of these texts is that the Messiah has not yet come and will only come when Jewish obedience reaches a high level of obedience, but the standard Christian view is that the Messiah came in the first century CE, 700 years after the time of Isaiah.

It is important to note that the Jewish Bible ends with the 39 books indicated in this chapter and the previous chapters. Further commentary on Jewish faith and practice is taken up in number of other works, including a set of books titled the Talmud, in which extensive rabbinic commentary on the Mosaic Law is given. However, Christians added directly to these 39 books, as they developed the book they would eventually call the "Bible". In the next chapter, commentary is given on how the second half of the Protestant Bible, known as the New Testament, was formed.

Chapter Seven
The Formation and Canonization of the New Testament

AS was noted in "Chapter Two", the canonization of the books of the Old Testament concluded a lengthy process of sorting and collecting ancient Israelite traditions, some of which were transmitted orally initially and some of which were transmitted in written form. Eventually all of the approved traditions were written and canonized in three distinct stages: the Torah, the Prophets, and the Writings.

The books of the New Testament also underwent a process of collecting and sorting. However this occurred over a much briefer period of time than what occurred in the process of the formation and canonization of the Old Testament. Written over a period of approximately 60 years, most of the books of the New Testament did not pass through an oral stage but were written down immediately. This is not true though for the first books of the New Testament.

Formation of Traditions

The books of the New Testament are focused mostly on the life and teachings of Jesus, who was born approximately 5 BCE and died approximately 30 CE according to Christian tradition. Most biblical scholars contend that traditions about Jesus were not written down during Jesus' lifetime nor were they written down shortly after his death. Rather scholars refer to a "tunnel period" in which traditions about Jesus were transmitted orally by his followers. Moreover, according to this view the traditions about Jesus initially were not organized into a complete biography of his life, but instead the traditions were communicated separately, with some traditions indicating his answers to religious questions and others indicating events and activities in his life.

Approximately forty years after Jesus' death,[1] the various traditions were collected and organized into biographies of Jesus' life called "Gospels". Based on the Greek word *euangelion*, the word Gospel means good news.

While the Gospels reflect events of Jesus' life that occurred around 30 CE, they were not the first New Testament books written. That honor goes to the letters of the Apostle Paul.[2] As is demonstrated in "Chapter Nine", the Apostle Paul traveled many miles to spread his message to the Gentile world. After starting churches in an area, he revisited the churches when possible, and he also wrote many letters to the churches, correcting them when they fell into wrong belief or practice and encouraging them to continue in the faith when they encountered persecution. Most scholars believe that Paul was the first one to write a document that was included in the New Testament. Beginning his missionary journeys around 47 CE, Paul wrote his first letter, the letter to the Galatians, a year later in 48 CE. Paul continued his ministry for another twenty years, probably writing hundreds of letters, thirteen of which have been included in the New Testament. Paul was killed by the Romans approximately 67 CE, so his letters must have been written prior to that date.

Presenting the history of the growth of the early church from a small group of Jewish followers of Jesus in Jerusalem to thousands of Gentile believers scattered across the Roman Empire, the book of Acts is the only historical narrative in the New Testament. Supposedly written by the author who also wrote the Gospel of Luke, this ancient document was probably written sometime in the 60s CE. Based on evidence within the book of Acts, it appears that its author joined Paul during his second missionary journey and was able to gain information about Paul's journeys first hand. However, the journeys of Paul only account for

---

[1] While some New Testament scholars believe the earliest biography of Jesus' life was written around 40 CE, most contend that it wasn't written until 70 CE.
[2] Based on two Greek words which mean "sent from", the title "apostle" was the title for an early Christian leader who claimed to have seen Jesus after his death. It was believed that apostles were able to perform miracles.

about half of the material in Acts. The rest of the material reflects the growth of the early church in Jerusalem under the leadership of the Apostle Peter. Hence, whoever wrote the book of Acts seems to have investigated what happened in the earlier years of the church. In fact, in the prologue to the Gospel of Luke, this author claims to have researched the historical basis for his work (see "Chapter Eight").

While it is plausible that some of the Gospels, all of Acts, and all of the Pauline letters were completed by 70 CE, the section known as the General Letters (see commentary in "Chapter Ten") and the last book of the New Testament titled the book of Revelation were probably not completed until the 90s CE. The General Letters consist of the Letter to the Hebrews (author unknown), the Letter of James, two letters of Peter, three letters of John, and the Letter of Jude.[3] Supposedly written by the youngest Apostle named John, the book of Revelation presents an early Christian understanding of the cosmic war between good and evil (see "Chapter Eleven" for commentary on Revelation).

As can be seen from the above commentary, the New Testament has a variety of books, 27 in total, including biographies about Jesus, an historical book, 13 letters of Paul, 8 General Letters, and the book of Revelation. The list of books is as follows:

Gospels	**Pauline Letters**	**General Letters**
Matthew	Romans	Hebrews
Mark	1-2 Corinthians	James
Luke	Galatians	1-2 Peter
John	Ephesians	1-3 John
	Philippians	Jude
	Colossians	
Historical	1-2 Thessalonians	**Apocalyptic**
Acts	1-2 Timothy	Revelation
	Titus Philemon	

---

[3] As is true of all of the books of the Bible, there are debates about the date and authorship of the General Letters. Some scholars believe the letters of James and Jude might have been written as early as the 50s C.E. and that 1-2 Peter might have been written in the mid-60s C.E.

While there is evidence to support the idea that most of the books in the New Testament were accepted as authoritative almost immediately after they were written, the process of the canonization of the New Testament was not completed by the end of the first century CE. One reason for the delay was perhaps due to the belief among the early Christians that the Holy Spirit was available to all of them and hence at any moment anyone among them might be inspired by God to speak revelatory words. Since God's guidance could be determined through an interpretation of these inspired words, Scripture was not viewed as something that could be closed. God's word was ongoing and actively spoken in the community of faith.

Reasons for Creating a Canon of Christian Scripture

However, by the middle of the second century CE, Christian leaders became concerned about developments that threatened their open approach to the Scripture. There seemed to be three main issues that caused Christian leaders to move toward a closed canon, including the following:

Intensified Persecution: While Christians faced persecution in the 60s and again in the 90s CE, they faced increased pressure in the second century. As New Testament historian Richard Niswonger notes:

> The Roman authorities viewed Christians as subversives who threatened the established social order. There is some evidence that despite the absence of a systematic crusade, there was an understanding by Roman leaders that Christianity was something more than just another branch of the legally approved religion, Judaism, but was in fact an illegal cult and that to be a Christian was per se a serious criminal offense.[4]

Not only were Christian lives in danger, but their sacred texts were threatened with destruction by the Roman authorities. The ever growing

---

[4] Richard Niswonger, *New Testament History* (Grand Rapids: Zondervan, 1988), 274.

number of Christian texts made it difficult for Christians to know which ones to attempt to hide from the Roman soldiers and which ones were of lesser quality, not worthy of risking one's life for.

Roman Soldiers

Competing Ideas about Christian Faith: The spread of Christian ideas and texts across the Roman Empire created a context for the borrowing of those ideas by individuals who interpreted them differently than the early apostles. One subset of Christianity was known as the Ebionites. These were followers of Jesus who believed Jesus was the Messiah but not God. They wrote several Gospels, such as the Gospel of the Nazoreans,[5] which supported their viewpoint. On the opposite end of the spectrum, there was another subset known as the Gnostics. They believed Christ was divine and not human. They believed Christ

---

[5] This Gospel is attested to by the church fathers, but no copy has been found.

descended from heaven, temporarily possessed the man named Jesus, spoke spiritual truths to the world, and then ascended back to God while Jesus died on the cross.[6] The Gospel that reflects their point of view was called the Gospel of Thomas.[7] The influences of these two groups alarmed Christian leaders who believed Jesus was both God and man. So they felt compelled to decide which early texts needed to be in the Christian canon and which ones needed to be excluded.

Proliferation of Christian Writings: Not only did influential Christian leaders become concerned about the existence of Gospels which did not reflect their belief and practice, but also they became concerned about the proliferation of Christian documents within their own context. There were so many significant leaders writing letters and sermons that it was becoming difficult for Christians to determine which documents should be consulted when it came to making important theological decisions. People didn't have the resources to make copies of every new scroll that was being produced. They needed to know what the primary texts were that had to be consulted.

Four Stages of Canonization

Due to the above issues, Christian leaders began a lengthy debate concerning which books to include in the New Testament and which ones to exclude. The development of the Christian canon seemed to involve four stages:

Quotations Used as Scripture: When Christian leaders faced questions raised by the community of faith, they wanted to give helpful answers which they believed reflected God's will. As such they

---

[6] It is difficult to summarize Gnostic beliefs, because there was a wide variety. Those who are interested in studying further in this area will find helpful commentary at http://www.newworldencyclopedia.org/entry/Gnosticism.

[7] Supposedly written by the Apostle Thomas, this document presents Jesus as a Gnostic philosopher who was a spiritual elitist, negative toward women. The Christian church fathers rejected this text, contending that it was not authentic. The entirety of this ancient document is now available on the internet.

attempted to base their answers on Christian texts they believed were inspired by God. Hence, they utilized quotations from those texts and incorporated them into their answers. Whenever an ancient Christian text was used in this manner by one of the early church fathers, the authority of the text being quoted was elevated.

Arguments for Accepted Books: As early texts circulated among the various Christian churches spread across the Roman Empire, some churches gravitated toward certain texts, while some churches emphasized other texts. The leaders in the churches reflected the views of their respective communities, arguing for the authority of some texts and against others. For example, leaders in churches in the western region of the Empire contended that the Letter to the Hebrews should be included in the Christian canon, because they maintained the letter was written by the Apostle Paul. However, leaders in the eastern region believed the letter should not be included. They did not believe Paul wrote it. The arguments for and against ancient books can be found in an early church history written by Eusebius.[8]

Making Lists: Eventually, leaders in the church began to make lists of books which they believed should be included in the New Testament. One of the earliest known lists was the Muratorian Canon.[9] Containing a list of 22 books (of which 21 eventually made it into the New Testament), this list was completed approximately 170 CE. By creating lists, early church leaders were attempting to solidify the canon, establishing both the number and order of the books. However, discussion and argumentation concerning which books to include continued for a lengthy period of time. While it only took about 60 years for the New Testament books to be written, it would take another 270 years before the canon was finally closed in 367 CE. Why did it take so long?

Church/State Connection: As long as Christians remained a persecuted minority under the authority of the Roman government, the

---

[8] For more information on Eusebius, see http://www.ntcanon.org/Eusebius.html.
[9] For more information on the Muratorian Canon, see http://www.earlychristianwritings.com/muratorian.html.

movement toward canonization was prolonged, because there was not a central authority that could make decisions that others would abide by. The debates within the Christian community were intense, and no one had the power to dictate which books would be included in the canon.

However, in the early part of the fourth century CE, the Roman Emperor Constantine stopped the persecution of Christians, and he inserted himself as its leader. He called for councils to meet to decide matters of doctrine related to Jesus' divinity, and those councils had the power of the state to make their decisions stick. About 40 years after Constantine made these changes, the canon of the New Testament was finalized.

Criteria for Canonization

While biblical scholars do not agree about the extent to which specific criteria were used in the creation of the Christian canon, according to early church documents the debate over which books to include in the New Testament seemed to be focused on four main issues or criteria for canonization:

Apostolicity: This criterion meant that a book had to be written by an apostle or someone who was working with an apostle. Contending that only books reflecting firsthand knowledge of the risen Christ should be considered authoritative, the church fathers anchored most of their arguments upon this criterion. A good example of how this criterion functioned is found in the discussion about the book of Hebrews. As was noted above, the western church maintained that Hebrews should be included in the canon, because Paul wrote it. However, the eastern church did not believe Paul wrote it, so leaders in the east felt the book should not be included in the canon. Eventually the arguments made by the western church won the day, and Hebrews was included in the canon.

Doctrinality: This criterion reflects the concern of the early Christian leaders that accepted books must support the beliefs which those leaders believed were doctrinally accurate. Since they rejected the beliefs of the Ebionites and the Gnostics (see commentary above), they also rejected their Gospels. Convinced that Jesus was both God and man in his nature, they did not accept Gospels that indicated otherwise.

Harmony: This criterion meant that a book had to be in harmony or agreement with other accepted books. In other words, once it was agreed that certain books should be in the canon, the ideas and themes within those books became the basis for examining other books. A good example of how this criterion functioned involves the decision the early church made about the Gospel of Thomas. Contending that this gospel clearly disagreed theologically with the other accepted gospels, church fathers maintained that this gospel could not have been written by the Apostle Thomas, and therefore, it could not be included in the New Testament.

Inspiration: Ultimately, the inclusion of books in the New Testament was based on the criterion that a book had to be inspired by God. Obviously, making a decision about whether or not a book was inspired by God would have been a highly subjective one. Nevertheless, it was the perspective of the early church fathers that all of the 27 books that finally made the canon were inspired by God.

Closing Comments

The complexity of the process of the canonization of the New Testament and the existence of Gospels that did not make the canon has led some scholars to question the reliability of the canonical process. In fact, many critical scholars have contended that some of the non-canonical Gospels should be consulted when research about Jesus is undertaken. They believe the New Testament does not contain all of the necessary information. However, conservative scholars have responded that the canonical process evolved appropriately due to God's guidance, and therefore, the books in the New Testament are the most important and reliable sources for understanding Jesus.

Regardless of which approach one decides to take concerning the canonization of the New Testament, a study of the New Testament does reveal the intense passion of Jesus and his followers as they attempted to advance the concept of a peaceable Kingdom of God in the context of a violent world, and this is certainly obvious in the four canonical Gospels, which are the focus of the next chapter.

Chapter Eight
The Gospels

AS was noted in the previous chapter, the Gospels are biographies about Jesus, a Jewish carpenter living in the first century CE. Much has been written about Jesus, with some scholars contending that he left behind his humble beginnings and became a wandering philosopher who ultimately had little impact on his society. Yet, others contend that he was and is the Son of God who has provided all humans with a pathway to eternal life.

Debates about the significance of Jesus are often divided into several periods called "Quests for the Historical Jesus". Beginning in the late 1700s, the quests for the historical Jesus involved attempts by critical scholars to separate passages within the Gospels that accurately represent what Jesus said and did from passages which were created by later Christians who believed Jesus was the Son of God. In response, conservative scholars have protested the goal of these quests, contending that the quests are too speculative, because they attempt to identify layers within the Gospels that originally did not exist.

Authorship of the Gospels

To some extent, the debate over the accuracy of the Gospels depends on who wrote them. Many conservative biblical scholars contend that the Gospels were written by those for whom the gospels were named, and therefore they maintain that: a) the Gospel of Matthew was written by Matthew, a disciple of Jesus and later an apostle in the early church; b) the Gospel of Mark was written by Mark, a close associate of Peter, who also was a disciple of Jesus and later an apostle; c) the Gospel of Luke was written by Luke, a close associate of Paul, who was an apostle to the Gentile Christians; and d) the Gospel of John was written by John, another disciple and later an apostle. According to scholars coming from this perspective, the Gospels were written by those who were close to Jesus or who knew someone who was a disciple. Therefore, the Gospels accurately represent what Jesus said and did.

However, critical biblical scholars have another perspective. They contend that the titles of the Gospels (e.g., "the Gospel according to Matthew") were added later to early copies and that it is impossible to know who actually wrote them. Yet, they do contend that it is possible, based on a close reading of the documents themselves, to make educated observations about how the Gospels were formed and how they might be related to each other. They maintain that a comparison of the Gospels reveals that Matthew, Mark, and Luke are very similar and are probably interrelated, while the Gospel of John is much different and most likely not related to the first three. According to this perspective, the authors of the Gospels of Matthew and Luke utilized the narrative framework in the shorter Gospel of Mark, and then they added material from another hypothetical written source which they have titled "Q",[1] which was an early source containing mostly wisdom sayings of Jesus.

Because the first three Gospels are so tightly interrelated, they have been called the "**Synoptic**" Gospels, referring to the practice of placing the three Gospels "side-by-side" to demonstrate their similarities. Concerning the Gospel of John, many critical scholars are not convinced that it is historically accurate. Contending that this Gospel is very different from the Synoptic Gospels and that its portrayal of Jesus is elevated spiritually far above the portrayals in the Synoptic Gospels, critical scholars contend the Gospel of John was written by members of a Gentile church who saw Jesus more as a heavenly figure guiding them toward eternal salvation rather than as a Jewish teacher who tried to stop his people from going to war with Rome, as is reflected in the Synoptic Gospels.

---

[1] The letter "Q" is used, because it is an abbreviation of the German word "Quelle" which means "source".

The Literary Form of Gospel

As was noted above, Gospels primarily are biographies of the life and teachings of Jesus.[2] However, the Gospels were not written like biographies of today, which are in an essay style. Rather, Gospels were written in a narrative form, with setting, plot, characters, and point of view. Therefore, what was stated in "Chapter Three" concerning the analysis of historical narratives holds true for the analysis of Gospels.

Yet, there are also some distinctive elements within the Gospel narratives which need to be taken into consideration, including the following:

Centrality of Jesus: While historical narratives shift focus and have several important characters, in the Gospels the different elements are there to highlight some aspect of Jesus' life. Many of the characters in the Gospels are not given names and are in only one scene, functioning as foils, emphasizing one aspect of Jesus' life. Even the close followers of Jesus are not well developed characters in the text. They are confused and disoriented much of the time. So an analysis of a Gospel text involves commenting on what the text has to say about Jesus. Hence, Gospels are overtly evangelical. They are attempting to convince the reader that Jesus was and is the Messiah who died for the sins of humanity.

Loosely Connected Narrative Units: In historical narratives, narrative units begin with an introduction to a new character, scene, and/or idea, continue with closely related events, and conclude with a summary statement. In the Gospels, narrative units normally do not have a summary statement at the end of the units. The narrative units rarely are connected by a transitional statement. This means the narrative units are often simply placed side-by-side, making it more difficult for the

---

[2] There is a debate among scholars concerning how to identify the literary form called "gospel". Options for understanding a gospel as a literary form include biography, memoir, or narrative. Certain scholars contend that Gospels are so loosely constructed that they are not a literary form in and of themselves, but rather they contain disorganized traditions about Jesus.

reader to know when one narrative unit has ceased and another has started.

Embedded Subgenres: While most of the passages in a Gospel are written in narrative form and are focused on presenting some aspect of Jesus' life, there are passages in the Gospel which are not in narrative form, including: a) genealogies presenting Jesus' ancestry; b) quotations from the Old Testament that are connected to an aspect of Jesus' life; c) narrator explanations in which the author of a Gospel explains the significance of something Jesus said or did; d) lengthy sermons in which Jesus' thoughts about a variety of topics are presented; and e) parables (simple stories with a deeper spiritual truth[3]) within Jesus' answers to often complex or controversial issues. When a reader is analyzing a Gospel passage, it is important for the reader to identify the embedded subgenres and determine what the function of each subgenre is. In this regard, it is necessary for the reader to determine what leads into the subgenre and what follows. The best clues for interpreting a passage, especially a passage with a subgenre, are found within the immediate context of a passage.

In many ways, the Gospels are deceptive for the beginning reader. Since Jesus is clearly the protagonist in the text and the conflicts driving the plot are fairly obvious, some readers mistakenly believe Gospel texts are easy to read. However, as was noted above, there are many aspects in a Gospel that a reader needs to keep track of including how the passage reflects an event in the timeline of Jesus' life, what that event indicates

---

[3] According to the Gospels, Jesus often used parables when he was speaking to the common people, because he could use agricultural images that they understood in order to convey spiritual truths. For example, Jesus told a parable about how some people would understand his message and some would not. In this parable, Jesus compared himself to a farmer who was planting a field. When the farmer sowed the seed in good soil, then a crop would grow. However, when the farmer inadvertently had seed fall on rocky soil or among weeds, then the crop would not come up. In the same way, those who have hard hearts would not be able to produce a deeper spirituality even if they heard a good sermon. According to the Gospels, Jesus also used parables when addressing questions from religious authorities who wanted to trap Jesus in an answer that would get Jesus in trouble with the authorities.

about Jesus, and whether or not an embedded subgenre exists within the passage providing non-narrative commentary on Jesus' significance.

An example of a Gospel passage which has an embedded subgenre is found in Mark 1:

> The beginning of the good news of Jesus Christ, the Son of God. As it is written in the prophet Isaiah, 'See, I am sending my messenger ahead of you, who will prepare your way; the voice of one crying in the wilderness: "Prepare the way of the Lord, make his paths straight,"' John the baptizer appeared in the wilderness, proclaiming a baptism of repentance for forgiveness of sins. And people from the whole Judean countryside and all the people of Jerusalem were going out to him, and were baptized by him in the river Jordan, confessing their sins....In those days Jesus came from Nazareth of Galilee and was baptized by John in the Jordan. And just as he was coming up out of the water, he saw the heavens torn apart and the Spirit descending like a dove on him.[4]

In this passage, a quotation from the Old Testament is given,[5] but it is not explained. After the quotation, the author of Mark's Gospel jumps into the narrative, telling first about John the Baptist and then about Jesus being baptized by John. In order to determine what the function of the Old Testament quotation is, the reader must consider it within its context. The immediate context is that John has been baptizing people as they repent of their sins. This seems to be connected to the portion of the prophecy indicating that a messenger was preparing a way for "you". The question is: who is this referring to? Once again the context is helpful. Jesus was baptized by John, and God demonstrated approval of Jesus by sending the Spirit upon Jesus. Hence, the literary evidence is that John was preparing the way for Jesus. This interpretation also makes

---

[4] Mark 1:1-5, 9-10.
[5] While the author of Mark's Gospel indicates the passage is from the book of Isaiah, an examination of the quotation reveals that it was drawn from several sources including Isaiah 40; Exodus 23; and Malachi 3.

sense in light of the fact that Gospels are biographies of Jesus. Jesus is the focus.

Content of the Gospels

Given the gap that exists between conservative and critical scholars concerning who Jesus was, it is all the more important for interested individuals to read the Gospels for themselves. What they will find is that the Gospels agree on certain key events, and also have key emphases, making each Gospel distinct.

Concerning events upheld by all of the Gospels, each Gospel writer apparently felt that it was necessary to indicate that Jesus was raised in Nazareth, a city in northern Israel in an area called Galilee where Jesus did most of his ministry.

Hills of Northern Galilee

Also, each Gospel writer referred to: a) Jesus calling twelve men to be his disciples whom Jesus trained for ministry; b) Jesus being baptized by a prophet named John in preparation for Jesus' ministry; c) Jesus performing miracles such as healing, raising people from the dead, casting out demons, and altering elements of nature; d) Jesus proclaiming a powerful message about God's love for all people, including tax collectors, sinners, and Roman soldiers; e) certain religious and political groups opposing Jesus' efforts; f) eventually Jesus traveling to Jerusalem where he was betrayed by one of his disciples, arrested by the keepers of the Temple known as the Sadducees, and finally tortured and killed by Pontius Pilate, the Roman governor; and g) Jesus rising from the dead and encouraging his disciples to continue the ministry work which Jesus had started.

Concerning distinctive elements within each Gospel, there are several worth noting, including the following:

Gospel of Matthew (written approximately 80 CE):[6] In Matthew's Gospel, Jesus is presented primarily as a great teacher and interpreter of the Scripture who believed obedience to God did not involve an austere legalism but rather an internalization of the teachings contained within the Old Testament. According to Matthew, Jesus believed it was not enough to avoid murdering your neighbor. You also needed to avoid hating your neighbor. In fact, Jesus called for everyone to love their neighbor, including those who were enemies. In five great sermons scattered throughout this Gospel, Jesus spoke about spiritual devotions (such as charity, prayer, and fasting), the pathway to eternal life (narrow is the way), the mission of his disciples, parables of the Kingdom of God, how to handle problems within the community of faith, the need to avoid false teachers, the importance of caring for the poor, and warning signs indicating the end of time.

Gospel of Mark (written approximately 60 CE): Considered by most biblical scholars to be the first Gospel written, this Gospel is action oriented and contains only a few of Jesus' teachings. Apparently

---

[6] The approximate dates given for the writing of the Gospels in this section are based on the views of conservative scholarship.

attempting to demonstrate the powerful nature of Jesus' ministry, the author of the Gospel of Mark overwhelms the reader as Jesus overcomes temptation, calls his disciples, casts out a demon, and heals the sick, all in the first chapter! The supernatural power of Jesus is emphasized in other sections of Mark's Gospel as well, as Jesus feeds the multitudes and walks on water during one of his crossings of the Sea of Galilee.

The Sea of Galilee

After pushing the reader through key events in Jesus' ministry, at the end of the Gospel the author described Jesus' final days in graphic terms. Jesus was arrested while praying in a garden. He was falsely charged by religious authorities who were intimidated by Jesus' influence with the common people. He was brutally whipped and then had a crown of thorns shoved on his head by Roman soldiers. He was condemned to death by a reluctant Pontius Pilate who saw something in Jesus that Pilate apparently had not seen in many others that he had sentenced to death. Jesus was then crucified on a cross, the Roman way of killing messianic pretenders. But according to Mark's Gospel, Jesus did not stay dead. After three days, he arose. He re-gathered his disciples and sent them out to evangelize the world.

Gospel of Luke (written approximately 65 CE): Primarily focused on Jesus' concern for disenfranchised people, the author of the Gospel of Luke presented key aspects of Jesus' life and teachings that are not contained in the other Gospels. For example, it is only through the Gospel of Luke that the reader has access to Mary's thoughts about the conception of Jesus, her son. Moreover, only Luke's Gospel indicates that Jesus was supported by wealthy women during his ministry. Hence, in Luke's Gospel women have a much more prominent role than in the other Gospels.

Not only does Luke's Gospel emphasize the significance of women in Jesus' life, but this Gospel also indicates Jesus' tremendous compassion for the lost and for the poor. This emphasis is obvious in certain parables uttered by Jesus in the Gospel of Luke. For example, there are several parables indicating God's concern for the lost, including the parables of the Lost Coin, the Lost Sheep, and the Prodigal Son.

Concerning Jesus' compassion for the poor, one of the most powerful parables in all of the Gospels is the Parable of the Rich Man and Lazarus. According to this passage (located in Luke 16:19-31), Jesus said:

> There was a rich man who was dressed in purple and fine linen and who feasted sumptuously every day. And at his gate lay a poor man named Lazarus, covered with sores, who longed to satisfy his hunger with what fell from the rich man's table; even the dogs would come and lick his sores. The poor man died and was carried away by the angels to be with Abraham. The rich man also died and was buried. In Hades, where he was being tormented, he looked up and saw Abraham far away with Lazarus by his side. He called out, "Father Abraham, have mercy on me, and send Lazarus to dip the tip of his finger in water and cool my tongue; for I am in agony in these flames." But Abraham said, "Child, remember that during your lifetime you received your good things, and Lazarus in like manner evil things; but now he is comforted here, and you are in agony.

> Besides all this, between you and us a great chasm has been fixed, so that those who might want to pass from here to you cannot do so, and no one can cross from there to us." He said, "Then, father, I beg you to send him to my father's house—for I have five brothers—that he may warn them, so that they will not also come into this place of torment." Abraham replied, "They have Moses and the prophets; they should listen to them." He said, "No, father Abraham; but if someone goes to them from the dead, they will repent." He said to them, "If they do not listen to Moses and the prophets, neither will they be convinced even if someone rises from the dead."

In this passage, a concern for the poor and a warning to the lost are combined. Drawing a connection between the two, Jesus indicated that people are responsible for their neighbors and that proper standing before God is based on the extent to which people take care of the poor. This concept is repeated throughout the Gospels, and it also is found in many of the Prophetic Books in the Old Testament.

Gospel of John (written approximately 95 CE): Written perhaps more than ten years after the last Synoptic Gospel was written, the Gospel of John has significant differences from the other three Gospels. While in the Synoptic Gospels Jesus appeared reluctant to say much about himself and even attempted to silence those who praised him for his miracles, according to the Gospel of John, Jesus was very open and overt about who he was and is, as can be seen from the following passages from the Gospel of John in which Jesus spoke about himself:

> I am the bread of life. Whoever comes to me will never be hungry, and whoever believes in me will never be thirsty.[7]

> I am the good shepherd. The good shepherd lays down his life for the sheep.[8]

> The Father and I are one.[9]

---

[7] John 6:35.
[8] John 10:15.

> I am the resurrection and the life. Those who believe in me, even though they die, will live, and everyone who lives and believes in me will never die.[10]

Critical scholars contend the elevation of Jesus in the Gospel of John was due to the imagination of a Gentile Christian community which wanted to present Jesus as the Son of God. However, conservative scholars disagree. One segment of conservative scholarship contends that the "I am" statements in John's Gospel are historically accurate, and that the reason only John's Gospel contains the statements is that it is the insider's Gospel, written to communicate Jesus' deeper thoughts to the Christian community. Another segment of conservative scholarship agrees that the sayings are accurate, but scholars coming from this point of view contend that the sayings reflect what Christians were hearing from the heavenly Jesus, who was speaking to them through their prayers.

Regardless of what one chooses to believe about the Gospel of John, it is important to note that Christians consider this Gospel to be one the most important documents in the New Testament, because it makes the strongest statements about Jesus' origin (he was with God since the beginning of time), his relationship to God (he is both God's Son as well as one with God), and his relevance for this world (he is its savior).

Concluding Comments on the Gospels

While the Gospels generally agree on key events in Jesus' life, there is a significant difference between passages concerning what is emphasized. For example, numerous passages in the Synoptic Gospels emphasize Jesus' humanity. Before he was crucified, Jesus experienced suffering, and he seemed to embrace it as a pathway to God. Contending that the violence of his world was contrary to God's kingly rule, Jesus

---

[9] John 10:30.
[10] John 11:25-26.

called for his disciples to love their enemies. Moreover, knowing that his popularity would eventually bring him into conflict with the political and religious authorities, Jesus foretold that the time would come when he would be crucified, and he asked his disciples to follow in his footsteps. They were to take up their crosses and follow Jesus into a new spiritual paradigm in which love conquers hate.

However, the Gospel of John emphasizes Jesus' divinity. While there are a few texts in the Synoptics which present Jesus in an elevated fashion, most of the passages indicating that Jesus was one with God are found in the Gospel of John (see commentary above). According to these texts, not only was Jesus the Messiah, but he also was and is the Son of God who was with God before all time. Then, after Jesus descended to earth, became flesh, and died on the cross for the sins of humanity, he ascended back to heaven from which vantage point he reigns over the whole universe, second only to God, his Father.

The books that follow the Gospels continue to comment on Jesus' significance. Even the timeline of Jesus' life does not end with the Gospels, but it is extended by the next book of the Bible, the book of Acts. As can be seen in the next chapter, the book of Acts indicates that Jesus re-gathered his disciples after his death/resurrection and that those disciples, along with the Apostle Paul, then spread a message about Jesus throughout the Roman Empire.

Chapter Nine
Acts and the Pauline Letters

THE book of Acts picks up where the Gospels leave off. According to the book of Acts, after Jesus was raised from the dead, he appeared to his disciples on a number of occasions. Along with assuring them that he had not abandoned them, Jesus also directed his disciples to wait in Jerusalem until God sent the Holy Spirit upon them, thereby giving them courage to take their message about Jesus to the world. The early disciples attempted to fulfill this mission, but they ran into opposition from certain religious leaders, including a man named Saul, whose Greek name was Paul. According to information in some of Paul's letters and in the book of Acts, Paul persecuted the early believers in Jesus until one day when Paul had a religious experience that convinced him that he had been wrong. From that day onward, Paul began to proclaim Jesus as the Christ, the savior of the world.

What Paul actually experienced that day is debated among scholars. Some scholars believe the book of Acts is historically accurate and hence reliable for reconstructing what happened to Paul. However, others are not convinced. They contend that most of Acts is fictitious. Once again the division among scholars concerning an interpretive issue is based upon a disagreement about who wrote key documents in the New Testament.

Authorship of Acts and the Pauline Letters

The opening of the book of Acts provides supporting evidence for the view that whoever wrote the Gospel of Luke also wrote the book of Acts. Consider, for example, the following passages from Luke and Acts:

> Since many have undertaken to set down an orderly account of the events that have been fulfilled among us, just as they were handed on to us by those who from the beginning were eyewitnesses and servants of the word, I too decided, after investigating everything carefully from the very first, to write an orderly account for you, most excellent Theophilus, so that you may know the exact truth concerning the things about which you have been instructed.[1]
>
> In the first book, Theophilus, I wrote about all that Jesus did and taught from the beginning.[2]

As can be seen above, in both passages the writer refers to Theophilus, who was either the person who paid for the production of the Gospel of Luke and the book of Acts, or a metaphorical name referring to any believer in Jesus (in Greek, the word Theophilus means "lover of God").

Based on this evidence and the perspective of the early church fathers that both of these books were written by a man named Luke who became a traveling companion of Paul, conservative scholars are comfortable that the book of Acts was written by Luke around 62 CE. However, critical scholars contend the book of Acts contains historical errors and that whoever wrote it must have written the book later in the first century or early second century CE. According to this perspective, the author was an unknown church leader, who was trying to unite warring segments within the early church.

Concerning the letters of Paul, scholars also have a difference of opinion. While most scholars generally agree that some of the letters attributed to Paul are authentic (including Romans, 1 Corinthians, 2 Corinthians, Galatians, Philippians, 1 Thessalonians, 2 Thessalonians, and Philemon), they do not agree about the authenticity of all of them. Even though all thirteen Pauline Letters clearly state within the opening of each letter that Paul is the author, critical scholars contend that at least five of the thirteen are not authentic. Scholars coming from this

---

[1] Luke 1:1-4.
[2] Acts 1:1.

perspective contend that the letters to the Ephesians and Colossians are inauthentic because they contain concepts and ideas different from the authentic Pauline letters. They contend that the letters of 1 Timothy, 2 Timothy, and Titus are also inauthentic,[3] because the language, style of writing, and theology of these three letters are much different from the authentic Pauline letters. Yet, while scholars do not agree on which of the so called Pauline Letters were actually written by Paul, they do agree the letters in this set have a distinctive literary style.

Literary Form of Paul's Letters

In the first century CE, the Roman government had an advanced mail system. Utilizing fast horses and their riders (much like the pony express in the Old West in American history), the Roman government was able to move mail from one end of the empire to the other in about two weeks. Like letters today, letters in Paul's day had a standard format. The letters opened with a reference to the writer of the letter, the receiver of the letter, and the word "greetings", sometimes accompanied by a wish for good health. In the middle section was the body of the letter, followed by the closing, which was usually a simple "farewell".

The three-fold format of Greco-Roman letters in the first century CE can be seen in the letter sent by the church in Jerusalem to the Gentile churches in Asia Minor as given in Acts 15:23-29:

> The brothers, both the apostles and the elders (***senders***), to the believers of Gentile origin in Antioch and Syria, and Cilicia (***receivers***), greetings. (***body begins here***) Since we have heard that certain persons who have gone out from us, have said things to disturb you, and have unsettled your minds, we have decided unanimously to choose representatives and send them to you, along with our beloved Barnabas and Paul…For it seemed good to the Holy Spirit and to us to impose on you no further burden than these essentials: that you abstain from what has been sacrificed to idols and from blood and from what is

---

[3] These three letters are often referred to as the "Pastoral Letters".

strangled and from fornication. If you keep yourselves from these, you will do well. Farewell (***closing***).[4]

As an educated man, Paul would have been aware of the standard letter format. Yet, he chose to alter the format of his letters, expanding certain sections and adding two more sections. Concerning expansions, Paul extended the opening of his letters to include a blessing: "Grace to you and peace from God our Father and the Lord Jesus Christ."[5] The word "grace" in this context is understood to mean "unmerited favor", and the word "peace" reflects the normal Hebrew greeting "Shalom", which connotes harmony with others. Hence, with this additional phrase, Paul seemed to be extending forgiveness from sins and reconciliation with God to the readers of his letters. Paul also expanded the closing of his letters. Instead of simply writing "farewell", Paul included greetings from those who were with him, and he also asked those receiving the letter to send special greetings to people he knew in the church. Furthermore, Paul included a blessing or benediction in the closing, such as: "The grace of the Lord Jesus be with you. My love be with all of you in Christ Jesus."[6]

Concerning additional sections in the Pauline letters, after the opening of his letters, Paul normally added what scholars call his "thanksgiving section", which contains Paul's expressions of thanks to God for something that the receivers of the letter have done well. Some scholars believe the thanksgiving section contains clues about what Paul included in the subsequent body of each letter. In the body of his letters, Paul usually addressed matters of doctrine, directing the churches concerning what they should believe. Before the closing section of his letters, Paul often added a "moral instruction" section, in which Paul specifically addressed issues related to behavior. Although in certain letters, moral instruction is blended into the body of the letter as well.

---

[4] As was noted above, after the Jerusalem council met this letter was sent to guide Gentile believers concerning their religious practices.
[5] Rom 1:7.
[6] 1 Cor 16:23-24.

In summing up the format of the Pauline letters, most of them have the following five main parts:

1. **Opening**: Sender, receiver, blessing
2. **Thanksgiving section**: Expression of gratitude to God
3. **Body**: Comments on doctrine
4. **Moral instruction**: Comments on behavior
5. **Closing**: Greetings, benediction

Along with identifying the main parts, a reader of a Pauline letter also needs to be aware of the style with which Paul wrote his letters. His style of writing includes the following elements:

Extended Modification: Utilizing the style of writing of his day, Paul often went on tangents. While writing about one issue, he would decide to modify key phrases and clauses in a building block fashion. For example, consider the first seven verses in the letter to the Romans. While this is simply the opening of the letter containing the sender, receiver, and blessing, it contains much more, as demonstrated in the following sentence analysis:

Paul *(sender)*,
    a servant of Jesus Christ,
    called to be an apostle,
    set apart for the gospel of God,
        which he promised beforehand
            through his prophets in the holy scriptures,
            the gospel concerning his Son,
                who was descended from
                David according to the flesh
              and was declared to be Son of God
            with power according to the
                resurrection from the dead,
            Jesus Christ our Lord,
              through whom we have
              received grace and
              apostleship to bring about
              the obedience of faith among

> all the Gentiles for the sake of his name,
> including yourselves who are called to belong to
> Jesus Christ,
> to all God's beloved in Rome *(receiver)*
> who are called to be saints:
>
> Grace to you and peace from God our Father
> and the Lord Jesus Christ **(Pauline blessing)**.

Obviously, it could take Paul a long time to say "Hi".

Old Testament Quotations: Like other Jewish writers of his day, Paul liked to support his view with quotations from the Old Testament. Based on his extensive knowledge of the Old Testament, Paul blended long and short quotations into his comments on key issues such as his view of the nature of God and the way of salvation.

Greco-Roman Rhetoric: Paul's hometown, the city of Tarsus, had a school of rhetoric, and there is evidence in Paul's letters that he had some training along this line. Greco-Roman rhetoric involved a question/answer format in which a speaker or writer would ask a tough question about his own views and then answer that question himself. Paul utilized this technique on several occasions, including within the context of an argument that he was making concerning his view of salvation. In the letter to the Romans, Paul made the case that salvation was not dependent upon good deeds but faith alone. Sensing that some might take his argument too far, Paul stated what some might be thinking in the form of a question and then Paul responded to his own question. Notice, for example, the following passage: "What then are we to say? Should we continue in sin in order that grace might abound? By no means! How can we who died to sin go on living in it?"[7] When encountering Paul's use of rhetoric in his letters, readers need to pay particular attention to what precedes the rhetorical question, because the passage preceding the question contains the interpretive clues that

---

[7] Rom 6:1-2.

readers need to understand the meaning of the question and Paul's response to his own question.

Figures of Speech: In numerous passages in the Pauline letters, figures of speech as presented in "Chapter Five" are evident including: a) metaphors (e.g., "armor of God"[8]), b) similes ("like a child serving his father"[9]); and c) allusions (e.g., "the faith of Abraham"[10]). When a reader encounters figures of speech in Paul's letters, the reader needs to take time to unpack them, so that the depth of Paul's thought can be understood.

Embedded Subgenres: Just as the Gospels have embedded literary forms that go beyond a biography written in a narrative form, Paul's letters also have embedded subgenres. These literary forms include: a) autobiographical comments about events and beliefs in Paul's past life as a Jewish Pharisee; b) lists of vices and virtues indicating the behavior believers should avoid and the behavior they should practice; c) early Christian hymns praising Jesus for who he was or what he did; d) prophetic statements indicating what would occur in the future of the church; and e) confessions of faith in which concise statements about matters of belief were to be uttered aloud. Paul utilized these different forms to emphasize or support statements he made either in the body of his letters or in the moral instruction sections.

Given the various literary aspects of Paul's letters, it is obvious that doing an analysis of his letters requires some effort. After identifying the five main parts of his letters, the reader then needs to identify the main topics in the body of the letter, identifying the various literary features Paul used in the process of developing his ideas. It is only after identifying the literary elements of Paul's letters that the reader can begin to address what the main points of his letters are.

---

[8] Eph 6:10.
[9] Phil 2:22.
[10] Rom 4.

Content of Acts and the Pauline Letters

As was noted above, the book of **Acts** presents what happened to Jesus' followers after he ascended to heaven. After receiving the Holy Spirit, the disciples began to spread their message about Jesus. They began in Jerusalem. While some Jews believed the message, most did not. Concerned that the disciples were stirring up trouble in Jerusalem, the Sadducees responded by having Peter, the leader of the disciples, arrested. However, the persecution of the early believers in Jesus, who called themselves the "Way", did not stop them. Rather, it caused them to scatter throughout Israel and to the surrounding regions, spreading their message that Jesus was reigning at the right hand of God, and therefore, should be worshipped as the Messiah, the Son of God.

Concern about the influence of the "Way" was so profound among some religious authorities that they authorized certain individuals to seek out and arrest the followers of Jesus wherever they might be found. One such individual was a Jewish Pharisee named Saul. As was noted above, Saul had a profound religious experience that altered his perspective about Jesus. Before the experience, Saul was certain that the group known as the "Way" was deceiving people and that they needed to be stopped. However, after this religious experience, Saul changed his mind. What happened to him?

According to the book of Acts, he heard Jesus speak to him:

> Meanwhile Saul, still breathing threats and murder against the disciples of the Lord, went to the high priest and asked him for letters to the synagogues at Damascus, so that if he found any who belonged to the Way, men or women, he might bring them bound to Jerusalem. Now as he was going along and approaching Damascus, suddenly a light from heaven flashed around him. He fell to the ground and heard a voice saying to him, "Saul, Saul, why do you persecute me?" He asked, "Who are you, Lord?" The reply came, "I am Jesus, whom you are persecuting."[11]

---

[11] Acts 9:1-5.

The intensity of the light blinded Saul, and he had to be led to Damascus by his companions. There Saul, also known as Paul,[12] waited three days before a believer named Ananias came and healed him of his blindness.

According to Paul's letter to the Galatians, after Paul was healed, he travelled to Arabia for a time, returned to Jerusalem, and eventually went to Cilicia where his hometown of Tarsus was located. According to Acts and Paul's letters, Paul stayed in Tarsus for as long as ten years before he came to Antioch, Syria where he joined a fellowship of believers, Jews and Gentiles, who became known as Christians.[13] Apparently inspired by what he encountered there, Paul decided to spread the message further west, and he began the first of his three great missionary journeys.

According to the book of Acts, the first journey involved Paul traveling to the island of Cyprus and then sailing to south central Asia Minor. After evangelizing the cities of Derbe, Lystra, and Iconium in the Roman province of Galatia, Paul returned to Antioch.

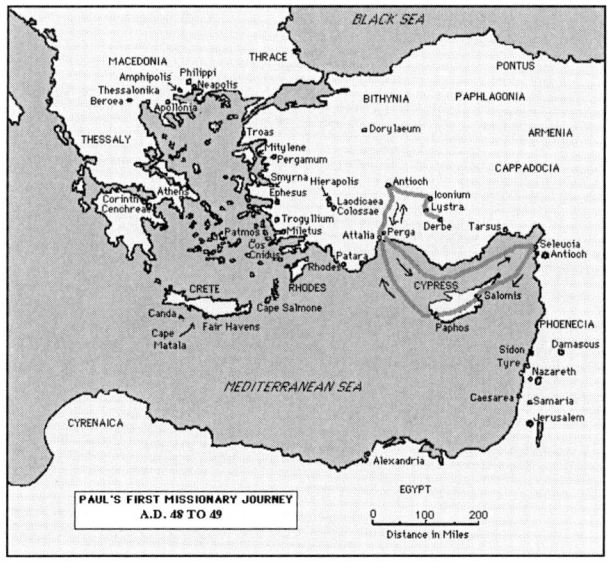

---

[12] Jews in Paul's day commonly had two names, a Jewish name and a Roman name. Hence, it is likely that Paul had both names from the time he was born.

[13] The first and only time the word "Christian" is used in the Bible is found in this context (Acts 11:26).

But there was a problem. Paul's success among the Gentiles created a controversy among the Jews, because they had heard that Paul was not upholding the Law nor the requirement of circumcision. In response to this concern, Paul attended a conference in Jerusalem in which he made the case that Gentiles could enter into the community of believers by faith and not by performing rituals or doing commandments according the Law of Moses. The church in Jerusalem mostly agreed with Paul. Requiring that Gentiles only avoid idol worship, eating blood, and fornication, the church wrote a letter (see quotation earlier in this chapter) that was sent to the Gentiles indicating its decision. Paul could continue his work unhindered.

In Paul's second and third missionary journeys, he traveled to western Asia Minor, Macedonia, and Greece, stopping at key cities along the way, creating new churches wherever he was received.

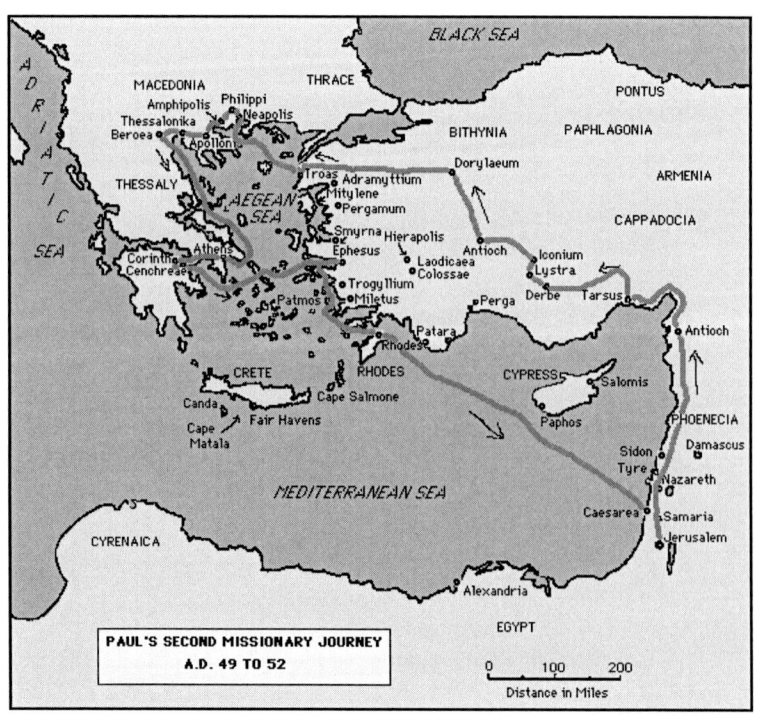

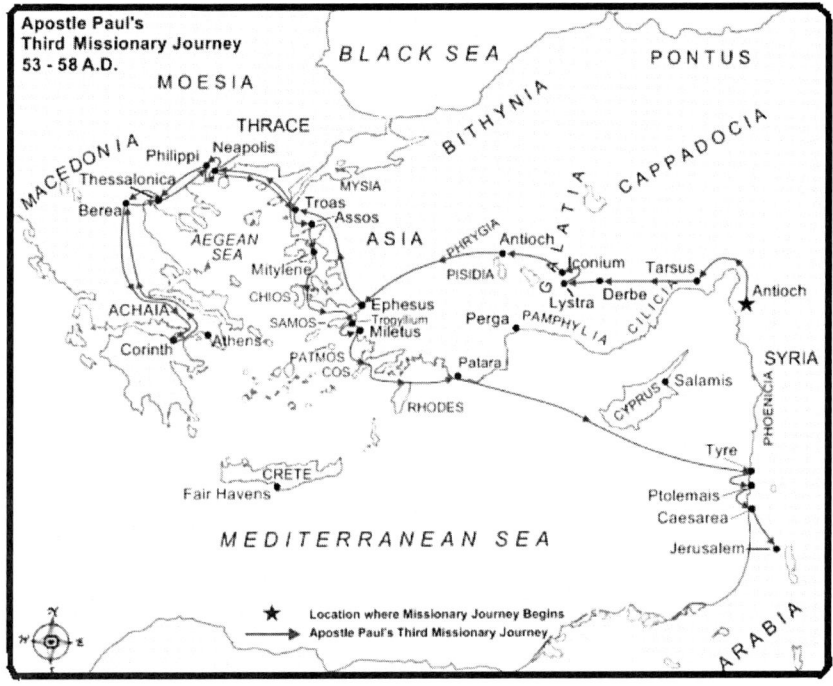

Paul's stated goal in his letters and in his speeches in Acts was to spread his message to new places, as far as he could go.

With all of his success in the Gentile world, he still felt the need to stay connected to the Jewish community. In each city that Paul visited, he began his ministry outreach by attending the local synagogue and proclaiming his message there. In the synagogues along with the Jews, Paul encountered Gentiles (called "God-fearers") who sat in a separate section and who were interested in the Jewish faith. While Paul was not very successful convincing his own people of this new message, many of the God-fearers were accepting of his message, and they provided Paul opportunities to speak to their Gentile neighbors.

The refusal by most of the Jews to refuse Paul's message was an ongoing frustration for Paul who felt the need to attempt to reconnect with his people. At the end of his third missionary journey, Paul traveled to Jerusalem in order to fulfill a vow by offering a sacrifice in the

Temple. However, when he attempted to enter the Temple area, he was recognized by some who were outraged that he would dare to come to the Temple after spending so much time among Gentiles. Paul would have most likely been killed by an angry crowd at that moment, but some Roman soldiers intervened and took him away. Because it wasn't safe for him in Jerusalem, Paul was taken to a prison at Caesarea Philippi, where he was kept for two years.

Since he didn't feel that he was going to get a fair trial in that city, Paul appealed to the king of the Roman Empire. As a Roman citizen, Paul had the right to receive a fair hearing, even if that meant standing before the Emperor himself. So Paul was placed on a ship which was headed toward Rome, but on the way a great storm arose, and the ship was destroyed. Paul and the other passengers survived by swimming to an island called Malta. The book of Acts closes with Paul living in Rome where he was under house arrest.

Based on their reading of sources in the early church fathers, some scholars contend that Paul eventually left Rome and travelled to Spain, where he continued his evangelistic efforts. These same sources indicate that after two years Paul decided to return to Rome when he heard the Christians were being tortured and killed by Roman authorities (see commentary on **2 Timothy**). When Paul returned to Rome, he was re-arrested, tried, and sentenced to death. He was beheaded outside of Rome.

It would be difficult to overstate the significance of Paul for the development of early Christianity. Not only did he spread the Christian message throughout the western regions of the Roman Empire, but he also wrote letters in which he presented profound theological concepts that became foundational for later Christian belief and practice. While Paul probably wrote numerous letters over the time of his ministry, only thirteen have been included in the New Testament. Focused mostly on issues of right belief and practice, the Pauline letters reflect Paul's pastoral concern for Christians in various cities in Asia Minor, Macedonia, Greece, and Rome. Brief summaries of each of his letters are given below.

Romans (written approximately 57 CE): Apparently placed first in the section containing the Pauline letters because it is the longest letter, the letter to the Romans is considered by many scholars to be Paul's most important letter. Written to Christians that Paul had not evangelized, Paul appeared to write the letter to introduce himself and his theology to the Romans, because he was hoping that they would support him in his mission to Spain.

Paul began his letter with his concern that both Gentiles and Jews have fallen short before God. Gentiles have fallen short, because although the work of the Creator should be obvious to them, they have chosen to worship things in the creation instead of the Creator. Jews have fallen short, because even though they have the advantage of having Scripture texts to guide them, they do not keep the commandments as they should. Therefore, both Jew and Gentile were in need of salvation.

In Paul's opinion, salvation has been provided through Jesus' atoning death on a cross. The word "atone" or "atonement" is a key theological word. Rooted in the idea of animal sacrifice in the Old Testament, Paul believed Jesus' death removed the penalty of death from all people. Jesus died in the place of sinful humans, taking upon himself the punishment they were supposed to experience. While God punished human sinfulness by eternal damnation, Paul believed people could be saved from this punishment by confessing with their mouth and believing in their hearts that Jesus was the Christ who died for them.[14] Once having received their salvation, believers could not have it taken from them by any power. Moreover, they were blessed with a special outpouring of God's spirit, and this enabled them to live a new life.

While confident that his beliefs were accurate, Paul did feel the need to address an issue that worked against his view that Jesus' death was for all people. In the latter half of the letter to the Romans, Paul acknowledged that most of the Jews in his day did not believe his message. If his message was correct and if the Jews were God's chosen people, then how could it be that they rejected Paul's message? Paul contended it was due to God's sovereignty. Paul made the case that God

---

[14] Rom 10:9.

chose to harden the hearts of the Jews for a time while God opened up salvation for the Gentiles. However, Paul also contended that the day would come when God would reverse his plan, and all of the Jews would be saved.[15]

1 Corinthians (written approximately 55 C.E.): This letter is a difficult one to read, because in it Paul confronted several serious problems that had developed among the Christians in the church at Corinth, a key city in Greece. One problem in the fellowship was that the Christians were arguing among themselves concerning who among them was the greatest. Another problem was that there was a man in their church who was committing adultery openly, and no one was taking the matter seriously. A third problem was that there were serious disputes among the Christians which they were not settling in the church, but instead they preferred to sue each other, taking the cases to secular courts. In response to these problems, Paul wrote to the Corinthians that: a) they were all members of the same body; b) they were empowered by the same Holy Spirit; c) they needed to be focused on love; and d) they needed to excommunicate believers who refused to repent of their sins. Paul concluded his letter by reminding them of the transforming power of his basic gospel message and how one day they would be transformed not only in the spirit but also in the body, because their bodies would be resurrected from the dead.

2 Corinthians (written approximately 56 CE): Apparently, some of the Corinthians were not very happy with Paul's command that one of the members of their church be excommunicated for committing adultery. Attempting to reconcile with those who were upset, Paul wrote this letter to reconnect with the Corinthian believers. As such, Paul commented on how he felt he had treated them respectfully and with integrity. Moreover, he reminded the Corinthians that he believed all believers were made new creatures when they accepted Christ as their savior. Hence, they were no longer sinners, but ambassadors for God, pleading with the unbelieving world to accept the gift of salvation.

---

[15] Rom 11:26.

Yet, while Paul was attempting to reconcile with the Corinthians, he still felt the need to justify his authority over them. So in the latter part of the letter, Paul wrote extensively of his concern for them and how much he had suffered as an apostle:

> Three times I was shipwrecked; for a night and a day I was adrift at sea; on frequent journeys, in danger from rivers, danger from bandits, danger from my own people, danger from Gentiles....in toil and hardship, through many a sleepless night, hungry and thirsty, often without food, cold and naked.[16]

For Paul, the primary sign of his apostleship was his suffering. He had paid a dear price to gain the authority that he had in the church.

Galatians (written approximately 48 CE): Although this is not the first Pauline letter canonically, it is chronologically. Many scholars maintain that this letter was written shortly before the Jerusalem council in which the church decided that Gentiles did not have to be circumcised (see commentary above). Paul's letter to the churches in the province of Galatia (south central Asia Minor) focuses mostly on Paul's concern that the Gentile believers were not holding firmly to the message that Paul had preached to them. Rather, Paul was afraid that they were being told by someone who had come into their midst that they needed to be circumcised and to keep all of the laws of the Mosaic Covenant in order to be saved. Paul staunchly disagreed with this approach. While Paul expected them not to abuse their spiritual freedom by committing sinful acts which Paul referred to as deeds of the flesh,[17] he didn't believe they could earn their salvation through the works of the law. Instead, he contended that salvation could not be gained by keeping the Law, but it could be gained by believing in Jesus who redeemed humanity from their sins through his death on a cross. So Paul wrote this letter to correct the Galatians and to remind them of the message that Paul preached to them while he was in their midst.

---

[16] 2 Cor 11:24-27.
[17] Gal 5:19f.

Ephesians (written approximately 61 CE): This is one of the letters that Paul wrote in prison. The letter to the churches in Ephesus is considered by many New Testament scholars to be second only to the letter to the Romans in terms of presenting Paul's theology. According to the opening portion of the letter, Paul indicated that God's plan from the beginning of time was to save the world through Christ, to whom had been given dominion and power over all spiritual forces. According to Paul, those who experienced the salvation that was available through Christ were joined together regardless of ethnicity, so that they might experience the mysterious wonder of God's plan and become people who make the world a better place, including improved relationships between husbands and wives, children and parents, and masters and slaves.

Paul concluded his letter by warning the Ephesians that they were in the midst of a spiritual war, and therefore, they needed to put on spiritual armor:

> Therefore, take up the whole armor of God, so that you may be able to withstand on that evil day, and having done everything, to stand firm. Stand firm therefore, and fasten the belt of truth around your waist, and put on the breastplate of righteousness....With all of these, take the shield of faith, with which you will be able to quench all the flaming arrows of the evil one. Take the helmet of salvation, and the sword of the Spirit, which is the word of God.[18]

Philippians (written approximately 58 CE): This is another prison epistle, and in it Paul indicated to the Philippians that he was very weary and longed for the day when he would be in heaven:

> For to me, living is Christ and dying is gain. If I am to live in the flesh, that means fruitful labor for me; and I do not know which I prefer. I am hard pressed between the two: my desire is to depart and be with Christ, for that is far better; but to remain in the flesh is more necessary for you. Since I am convinced of

---

[18] Eph 6:13-14, 16-17.

this, I know that I will remain and continue with all of you for your progress and joy in faith.[19]

In the ancient world, prison conditions were deplorable, with dirt floors covered in straw, no blankets, little light, horrible food, little water, and no toilets. Having spent several years in prison and probably not in the best of health due to all of the suffering he had experienced at the hands of political and religious authorities (see commentary on 2 Corinthians above), Paul expressed his struggles to the Philippians.

But he did not stay in that mindset. Rather, he continued in the letter to express his view that humility was the pathway to unity in the fellowship of believers. In his opinion, putting the interests of others ahead of self created a context for deep care. Not only was Paul an example of this type of humility (as demonstrated by his willingness to suffer in prison and his willingness to let go of the status he had achieved as a scholar in the Jewish community),[20] but also Paul indicated that Jesus demonstrated this type of humility by his willingness to suffer the ultimate shame of death on a cross.[21] As he moved to the end of his letter, Paul indicated that humility and suffering were the foundation for tremendous joy:

> Rejoice in the Lord always; again I will say, Rejoice. Let your gentleness be known to everyone. The Lord is near. Do not worry about anything, but in everything by prayer and supplication with thanksgiving let your requests be made known to God. And the peace of God, which surpasses all understanding, will guard your hearts and your minds in Christ Jesus.[22]

---

[19] Phil 1:21-25.
[20] Phil 3:1-10.
[21] Phil 2:5-11. Many scholars believe this passage was based on a "Christ-hymn" which was sung by the early church. In this passage, Paul indicated that Jesus was originally with God in heaven, descended to earth, became a man, suffered on the cross, was taken back to heaven, and was highly exalted.
[22] Phil 4:4-7.

Colossians (written approximately 57 CE): Yet another of Paul's prison epistles, the letter to the Colossians was written to Christians in the church at Colossae, a city in western Asia Minor, fairly close to the city of Ephesus. Unlike most of the other churches referred to in Paul's writings, the church at Colossae was not started by Paul. However, Paul still kept track of the church, and according to this letter, apparently Paul had heard that the Colossians were being misled by false teachers who seemed to be focused on a belief in angels and on religious rituals promoting an austere lifestyle. In response to this development, Paul made the case that redemption from sin was only possible through faith in Christ, who according to Paul, was not only with God from the beginning of time but also had, through his death on the cross, cancelled out the penalty for human sin.

Paul continued in the second half of the letter to indicate that the salvation Christians gained by faith was the basis for a new life. They could "put on the new self",[23] thereby transforming their minds and renewing their hearts. If they allowed this to take place, then their relationships would dramatically improve, including husband/wife relationships, parent/child relationships, and master/slave relationships (very similar to instructions in Ephesians; see above).

1 Thessalonians (written approximately 50 CE): Considered by some scholars to be the second of Paul's letters in the New Testament canon, the first letter to the Thessalonians (i.e., the believers living in the city of Thessalonica in Macedonia) is focused on Paul's encouragement to the Thessalonians to hold on to their faith in the midst of persecution. Paul believed that the day would come when Jesus would return from heaven and gather his people to himself:

> For the Lord himself, with a cry of command, with the archangel's call and with the sound of God's trumpet, will descend from heaven, and the dead in Christ will rise first. Then we who are alive, who are left, will be caught up in the

---

[23] Col 3:10.

clouds together with them to meet the Lord in the air; and so we will be with the Lord forever.[24]

Based on an interpretation of this passage and several other related passages in the New Testament, many Christians believe Jesus will come again at the end of time.

2 Thessalonians (written approximately 51 CE): Written just a few months after 1 Thessalonians, 2 Thessalonians follows up on Paul's comments about Jesus' second coming. Apparently after receiving Paul's first letter, someone in the church at Thessalonica expressed concern that they might miss the second coming. In response to that concern, Paul wrote this second letter, and in it, Paul indicated that there were a series of events that would precede the second coming. First, a man of lawlessness would take over the world, setting himself up as God. Then, in awe of this man, many in the church would be deceived and follow the man of lawlessness. Some time later, Jesus then would come, destroy the lawless one, and gather his people. Hence, Paul contended that there would be several signs signaling the second coming. It would not be easy to miss.

1 Timothy (written approximately 63 CE): The first of several personal letters that Paul sent to individuals instead of churches, this letter was written to Paul's right hand man, Timothy, whom Paul met and converted on one of his missionary journeys. Having a Jewish mother and a Roman father, Timothy, like Paul, had his feet in two different worlds. As such, he would have understood the need to stay connected to the Jewish community while at the same time reaching out to the Gentile community. Yet, as important as his mixed ancestry was as a foundation for his ministry, Timothy was valuable to Paul mostly because Timothy was a man of faith who loved Paul. In return, Paul clearly loved Timothy and viewed Timothy as one of only a handful of people that Paul could trust.

In this letter to Timothy, Paul instructed his friend and traveling companion to promote order in the churches. In the church services, men

---

[24] 1 Thess 4:16-17.

were to pray appropriately and women were to keep silent. According to this letter, Paul believed that women should not have a teaching role in the church.

While there are several passages in Paul's letters that seem to agree with this perspective, Paul's letters are not consistent on the issue of women in ministry. In other passages, Paul seemed to support women in ministry, and he even mentioned several such women, including Phoebe,[25] Prisca,[26] and Junia.[27] Moreover, Paul indicated in several places in his letters that God did not make a distinction between genders, going so far as to state that "there is no longer male and female; for all of you are one in Christ Jesus."[28] Given the tension between passages in Paul's letters that seem to limit women's roles in the church and others which seem more open, it is not surprising that various Christian denominations disagree concerning whether or not women can be pastors. While some Christian denominations do not allow women to be pastors, in the more liberal denominations women are allowed to be pastors.

After presenting his perspective on the respective roles of men and women in church services, Paul continued his letter by highlighting the criteria for identifying leaders in the church. In this section Paul mostly focused on issues of character, indicating that a leader should be kind, respectful to others, and incorruptible. Then Paul warned Timothy about false teachers who would arise and attempt to mislead the church. In the latter part of the letter, Paul encouraged Timothy to use his gifts carefully, to be respectful to the various people groups within the church, and to be a person of great character: "But as for you, man of God, shun

---

[25] Rom 16:1. In this passage, Paul indicated that Phoebe was a deaconess.

[26] Rom 16:3. Along with her husband Aquila, Paul considered Prisca to be a fellow worker with Paul. In fact, he stated in one letter that she risked her life for Paul.

[27] Rom 16:7. While the earliest Greek manuscripts do not agree about whether or not Paul was referring to a woman named Junia or a man named Junias in this passage, there are important manuscripts which support a reading of Junia, and in this passage, it appears that Paul referred to her as an apostle.

[28] Gal 3:28.

all this (i.e., worldly pursuits); *instead* pursue righteousness, godliness, faith, love, endurance, gentleness."[29]

2 Timothy (written approximately 67 CE): Probably the last letter in the New Testament written by Paul, this letter is also the most personal. The background of the letter was that a great persecution had broken out against the church, and many believers left the faith. According to Roman historians, the Emperor Nero blamed the Christians in Rome for a great fire that had destroyed a significant portion of the city of Rome in 64 CE. For three long years, Christians were brutally tortured and killed.

At the time the persecution broke out, the available evidence suggests that Paul was in Spain. However, Paul did not stay away, but returned, and he was arrested in Rome. After being captured, he wrote this letter to his friend Timothy, and Paul encouraged Timothy to hold on to his faith. Paul reminded Timothy of the faith of Timothy's mother and grandmother and how Timothy was himself endowed with great faith. Therefore, Paul wanted Timothy to be brave in the face of persecution, hold fast to the gifts God had given him, continue in the learning that he had gained from the inspired Scripture, avoid wickedness of all kinds, and proclaim the message of salvation, doing the work of an evangelist.

Knowing that his time was short, Paul concluded his letter by noting that the time of his death had come:

> As for me, I am already being poured out as a libation, and the time of my departure has come. I have fought the good fight, I have finished the race, I have kept the faith. From now on there is reserved for me a crown of righteousness, which the Lord, the righteous judge, will give me on that day, and not only to me but also to all who have longed for his appearing.[30]

Titus (written approximately 64 CE): While there is not as much evidence about Titus as there is about Timothy, it appears that Titus served in a similar role as Timothy. Both Timothy and Titus were entrusted by Paul to visit churches and guide them through difficult

---

[29] 1 Tim 6:11.
[30] 2 Tim 4:6-8.

issues. While the word "supervisor" or "director" is not used in the New Testament in reference to Timothy and Titus' role in the church, either title would be appropriate. Working under the authority of the apostle, Timothy and Titus were willing to help churches whenever Paul asked. Hence, it is not surprising that many of the issues presented in the first letter to Timothy appear as well in the letter to Titus.

As was noted above, 1st Timothy contains instructions concerning the appointment of leaders within the church and instructions concerning how different groups within the church were to be treated. Both types of instructions also are in the letter to Titus, along with Paul's words of encouragement to Titus to hold fast to his faith, faithfully guide the churches, and avoid worthless debates about speculative issues.

Philemon (written approximately 58 CE): During one of Paul's imprisonments, Paul met a slave named Onesimus, who had run away from his master. Due to Paul's teaching and influence, Onesimus accepted Paul's gospel message. At some point in the conversation, Paul realized that he knew Onesimus' master, who was Philemon, a man whom Paul had also led into the faith. When the day came for Onesimus to be returned to his master, Paul sent this letter with him, indicating to Philemon that he should not mistreat Onesimus, but rather Philemon should accept him back as a brother:

> Perhaps this is the reason he was separated from you for a while, so that you might have him back forever, no longer as a slave but more than a slave, a beloved brother—especially to me but how much more to you, both in the flesh and in the Lord. So if you consider me your partner, welcome him as you would welcome me.[31]

It would be difficult to overstate the significance of Paul's comments in light of Paul's culture. Scholars contend that there were millions of slaves in ancient Rome, and since they were considered to be property of the owners, they could be disfigured or killed if they ran away. So in

---

[31] Phlm 15-17. The reason no chapter number is given for this reference is that Philemon only has one chapter. It is the shortest of Paul's letters.

Paul's intercession on behalf of Onesimus, Paul stated the unimaginable in his culture. A slave was not property, but a human being who should be cared for like a close relative, a brother. In the history of humanity, it would be another 1800 years before even enlightened cultures such as America would be able to embrace Paul's statements on human equality.

Concluding Comments on Acts and Paul's Letters

Paul's ministry and letters were foundational for the development of Christianity. It was Paul who worked tirelessly in the face of numerous obstacles to start churches across the Roman Empire. Moreover, it was Paul who solidified what the basic message about Jesus would include. While Paul focused on the importance of Jesus for the developing church, he didn't do so based on Jesus' teachings but rather based on Paul's interpretation of the significance of Jesus' death and resurrection. Contending that Jesus' death was an atoning sacrifice for the sins of the world and that Jesus' resurrection opened up the pathway for Jesus' followers to be raised from the dead, Paul carved out a new pathway to God. According to Paul's letters, acceptance of Paul's gospel message meant that the new believer would experience the transforming power of God's Spirit, thereby enabling the new believer to live a moral life that reflected God's nature. In so doing, the Christian or saint (as Paul liked to call a believer) was positioned to be an ambassador for the new faith, helping others to see God's love for a fallen world through the sacrifice of God's Son.

The foundation built by Paul through his ministry and letters became the basis for writers of later documents that were eventually canonized and placed into the New Testament. Some of those documents were letters and are part of the next section of the Bible, titled the General Letters, which are the focus of the next chapter.

Chapter Ten
The General Letters

AS the title of this section in the New Testament suggests, these letters were written by a variety of authors who addressed an assortment of issues, including whether or not animal sacrifices were to be performed by Christians, how Christians were to respond to persecution, what type of behavior Christians were to have, how Christians could stay in relationship with each other, and how Christians could identify and avoid false teachers. Apparently reflecting key issues of the church in the late first century CE, these letters are pastorally oriented, addressing matters of belief and practice.

Authorship of the General Letters

Unlike the Pauline letters, the General letters were written by several different authors. However, scholars are not in agreement who those authors were. Concerning the letter to the Hebrews, certain scholars believe Paul wrote it, but others disagree, contending that any number of prominent first century Christians could have written it, including Apollos, Prisca, Barnabas, or Luke. Given that the letter does not indicate who wrote it and that the evidence for authorship within the context of the letter is sparse, most scholars contend it is best simply to say modern scholarship doesn't know who wrote the letter.

Concerning the letter of James, the letter indicates that it was written by a man named James, but the letter is not clear who this James was. There are several figures named James in the New Testament who could have been the author including two disciples of Jesus and one of Jesus' brothers. While critical scholars think it is best to leave the question of authorship open, conservative scholars believe the available evidence points to the James who was Jesus' brother. According to the book of Acts, this James became the head of the church in Jerusalem for a time, and he was the one who led the Jerusalem council which decided that

Gentile believers did not have to be circumcised (see commentary in "Chapter Nine").

Concerning the two letters of Peter, conservative scholars are comfortable that there is overwhelming evidence within both letters to substantiate that Peter the apostle wrote the letter. However, critical scholars believe the letters are forgeries. Contending that a fisherman in the first century CE would not have been able to write letters as stylish as 1st and 2nd Peter, these scholars maintain that someone wrote in Peter's name in an attempt to make their letters more authoritative in the church.

Concerning the three letters of John, conservative scholars believe that language and style of the letters connect well with the Gospel of John, and therefore, they believe the Apostle John wrote the letters and the Gospel bearing his name. However, critical scholars contend that the Gospel of John as well as the letters of John arose out of a segment of Christianity which had a more elevated view of Jesus than the rest of the church. Hence, for these scholars, the Johannine letters do not reflect the view of a single person, but rather a community of faith that was struggling to maintain its identity in a complex world.

Concerning the last of the General letters, the letter of Jude, scholars are divided between those who believe this letter was written by another brother of Jesus named Jude and those who believe the letter is a forgery, written by someone pretending to be Jesus' brother.

Literary Form of the General Letters

There is an inconsistency among the General Letters when it comes to the format of the letters. While the letters of 1 Peter, 2 John, and 3 John have all three parts of a standard Greco-Roman letter (i.e., opening, body, closing), the remaining five letters are missing key sections. For example, the letter to the Hebrews does not have an opening, but it does have a body and a closing. Some scholars contend this letter was based on a Christian sermon and that the beginning of the letter contains the thesis of the sermon. According to this view, it wasn't until later that an editor added a closing to the letter.

While the Letter to the Hebrews is lacking an opening but has a closing, the Letter of James is just the opposite. It has an opening and a body, but no closing. Moreover, since the letter addresses a variety of topics in the body of the letter and these topics are not well connected to each other, some scholars contend that the body was originally based on several short sermons, called homilies, and that they have been more or less haphazardly thrown together. Hence, a later editor might have added the opening and then sent the letter to the believers.

A couple more of the General Letters have the two part structure like the Letter of James. Both 2 Peter and Jude have an opening and a body, but they are lacking a closing. Unlike the letters mentioned so far, the Letter of 1 John has only the body of the letter. Lacking an opening and a closing, this letter also reads like a sermon. Yet, while it might have been read in front of an audience, it is also possible that John wrote it as an open letter that was posted in the town square for everyone to read.

Given the range of formats present in the General Letters, readers need to analyze each letter carefully before making decisions about how each letter was constructed. While looking for the various stylistic features that are in the letters of the New Testament as demonstrated in "Chapter Nine", the reader of the General Letters also needs to be aware of how the structure of each letter creates a context for the content of each letter.

Content of the General Letters

As was noted at the beginning of this chapter, the General Letters cover a wide range of topics reflecting the concerns of the church in the latter half of the first century CE. A brief summary of each book is given below:

Hebrews (written approximately 68 CE):[1] There is a debate among New Testament scholars concerning whether or not this letter was written before or after the destruction of the Second Temple in 70 CE.

---

[1] All of the dates given in this section are based on conservative scholarship. Critical views of the authorship of these letters can be found in the introductions to the letters in *The New Oxford Annotated Bible*.

The scholars in favor of a later dating (i.e., after the Temple fell) contend that this letter makes more sense in light of the loss of the Temple, because in the letter the writer made the case that animal sacrifices were no longer necessary—Jesus' death on the cross was the final atonement. Hence, the Jewish people should not be concerned with trying to rebuild the Temple a third time. However, other scholars contend that the letter was written at the time the Temple was still standing, and that the writer of the letter was attempting to convince the Jews that they no longer needed to bring animal sacrifices to the Temple in order to be forgiven of their sins.

Regardless of what one might choose to believe concerning when the letter was written, it is clear from the text itself that the writer utilized a "before and after" motif in constructing his letter. Throughout the letter the writer defended his thesis that in times past God spoke through the prophets, but in the "last days" God has spoken through his Son, Jesus Christ. In an attempt to prove his point, the writer compared various aspects of Jesus' person and life with parallels from the Old Testament, including the following comparisons: a) Jesus, as God's son, was closer to God than the angels; b) Jesus was a greater leader than Moses; c) Jesus was a better priest than the Levitical priests; and d) Jesus was a better sacrifice than animal sacrifice.

Since the author of Hebrews believed that Jesus mediated a better covenant than the Mosaic covenant, the writer contended that all people should have faith in Jesus just as the saints of the Old Testament had faith in God. Throughout the letter, the author warned his readers of the serious nature of the decision they faced, and toward the end of his letter he stated: "See that you do not refuse the one who is speaking; for if they did not escape when they refused the one who warned them on earth, how much less will we escape if we reject the one who warns from heaven!"[2]

James (written approximately 47 CE): Perhaps the earliest document in the New Testament, this letter was written to Christians scattered all over the Roman Empire. Apparently concerned that Christians were

---

[2] Heb 12:25.

receiving more instruction in doctrine than behavior, James contended that Christians should not fool themselves into believing that their behavior didn't matter as long as they had faith. Rather, James warned that "faith without works is also dead."[3]

Interestingly, James used the same biblical character to make his case for works that Paul used in making his case for the importance of faith—Abraham. In chapter four of Romans, Paul stated that Christians were saved by faith apart from works and that Abraham was the key example of someone who had been saved by his faith. However, James contended that it was not faith alone that saved Abraham, but rather, it was faith with works that brought about Abraham's right standing with God:

> Was not our ancestor Abraham justified by works when he offered his son Isaac on the altar? You see that faith was active along with his works, and faith was brought to completion by the works.[4]

Because James seemed to contradict Paul's teaching, some scholars have contended that there was a deep division between the Jewish believers in the church and the Gentile believers. As was noted in "Chapter Nine", in the book of Acts there is reference to a council that took place in Jerusalem in which the church decided to address this developing division. According to Acts chapter 15, Paul made the case that Gentiles should not be required to keep the Mosaic Law and be circumcised in order to be saved. After some deliberation, the church, led by James (whom conservative scholars believe was the same person who wrote the letter of James), decided not to impose the Mosaic Covenant upon the Gentiles. While the Gentiles were encouraged to avoid idol worship, fornication, and consuming blood, they were not required to keep any other commandments. Along with keeping these requirements, all they needed was to have faith in Jesus

---

[3] Jas 2:26.
[4] Jas 2:21-22.

While the letter of James does not overtly challenge that decree, it is in tension with Acts in that this letter clearly presents the need for works with faith. Throughout the letter, James instructs his readers to do what is right, including: a) seeking Godly wisdom; b) avoiding temptation; c) being slow to anger; d) avoiding all wickedness; e) controlling the tongue; f) taking care of orphans and widows; g) being humble; h) avoiding confrontations; i) living in the moment; j) not making oaths; and k) confessing sins. Because the variety of topics addressed in this letter relate to behavior, some scholars call this letter a book of Christian wisdom.

1 Peter (written approximately 67 CE): As the unofficial leader of the disciples of Jesus, Peter was often credited with asking Jesus questions that no one else dared to ask. Moreover, Peter was the risk taker among the disciples, venturing out on to the stormy sea when, according to the Gospel of Matthew, he saw Jesus walking on the water. According to all of the Gospels, only Peter was brave enough to follow Jesus into the courtyard  of the priest who questioned Jesus about his activities. Hence, while Peter experienced failures when he was under duress,[5] at least he was willing to take leaps of faith when others played it safe.

Peter's leadership among the disciples eventually translated into his leadership as an apostle. According to the book of Acts, it was Peter who preached a sermon during the feast of Pentecost, and in so doing, he attracted 3000 new believers to the faith. Due to his renewed vigor and courage, Peter led the church in Jerusalem for a while before James took over (see comments above). According to Paul's letter to the Galatians,

---

[5] Peter began to drown after leaving the boat, and three times he denied that he knew Jesus when he was questioned in the courtyard of the priest.

Peter was in Antioch for a time, but he did not stay there. The early church fathers contend that Peter eventually traveled to Rome, where he assumed leadership of the church. While he was in Rome, a persecution of Christians took place (see discussion in "Chapter Nine"), and Peter was arrested. According to church tradition, Peter was killed approximately 68 CE by crucifixion.[6]

Conservative scholars contend that after Peter was arrested, he wrote two letters that eventually were canonized and included in the New Testament. The first of those letters, 1 Peter, focused mostly on how believers had been born again as they were cleansed by Jesus' blood. Since they were followers of Jesus, Peter reminded believers that they should not be surprised when they were persecuted. Jesus suffered due to injustice. His followers should expect the same treatment. Therefore, Peter encouraged the believers in Rome to hold fast to their faith, not allowing themselves to seek revenge for mistreatment but to practice the virtues of humility and kindness, loving one another to the end.

2 Peter (written approximately 68 CE): Written shortly after 1 Peter, this letter continues with some of the same themes, as Peter encouraged believers to be diligent in their faith, be sure of their calling by God, and avoid false teachers who had arisen during a time of persecution. In the midst of the challenges the believers faced, Peter reminded them of their need to be morally above reproach, being blameless and focused on kindness and love. Moreover, Peter encouraged them to ignore those who were mocking them about their beliefs, particularly their belief that the day would come when Jesus would come again, bringing about a new beginning. Toward the end of the book of 2 Peter, Peter wrote:

> But do not ignore this one fact, beloved, that with the Lord one day is like a thousand years, and a thousand years are like one day. The Lord is not slow about his promise, as some think of slowness, but is patient with you, not wanting any to perish, but

---

[6] According to church tradition, Peter requested that he be crucified upside down, because he didn't feel he was worthy to die in the same manner that Jesus died.

all to come to repentance. But the day of the Lord will come like a thief, and then the heavens will pass away with a loud noise, and the elements will be dissolved with fire, and the earth and everything that is done on it will be disclosed.[7]

Peter then concluded his letter by encouraging the believers to live holy lives, being at peace, growing in grace and knowledge, following the teaching of apostles like Paul whose letters they had read.[8]

1 John (written approximately 91 CE): As was noted above, critical scholars maintain that the three letters of John were written by anonymous members of a Johannine community of faith, but conservative scholars maintain that the youngest of the twelve apostles was responsible for writing both the letters of John as well as the Gospel of John. Yet, ascribing the letters to the Apostle John does not provide even conservative scholars with much information, because little is known about John's early life beyond a few references in the Gospels and the book of Acts.

According to these references, John was the youngest disciple and a part of Jesus' inner circle, which included John, Peter, and James. After Jesus' death, John worked with Peter in the Jerusalem church, but John was more of a follower of Peter than a partner. Not much is known about John after his involvement with Peter in Jerusalem. For over 50 years, there is little evidence of what John did. However, according to the book of Revelation, later in John's life he began to oversee the churches in Asia Minor, and it was in that role that he was persecuted by the Roman Empire (for more commentary, see "Chapter Eleven").

Concerning the writing of the three Johannine Letters, it appears that John was addressing division within the community of faith. In the first of his letters, John laid the foundation for his understanding of how a community of faith should function. Relying upon the "word of life", the members of the community should be in fellowship with each other. In order to overcome the forces at work which were creating division, the

---

[7] 2 Pet 3:8-10.
[8] According to 2 Peter 3:15-16, Peter knew about Paul's letters, commenting that they were difficult to understand.

believers needed to focus on: a) walking in the light; b) confessing their sins; c) keeping God's commandments; d) loving one another; e) avoiding things of the world; f) practicing righteousness; g) abiding in the truth; and h) avoiding false teachers. John clearly hoped that his letter would either mend the division between believers or it would cause the false believers to depart, leaving a pure remnant in the church.

2 John (written approximately 92 CE): Referring to himself as "the elder", John wrote this letter to a church most likely in Asia Minor, where John was doing his work as an apostle. In this short letter, John re-emphasized some of the themes he wrote about in 1 John, including the need to walk in the light, love one another, and avoid false teachers.

3 John (written approximately 92 CE): Once again, John referred to himself as the elder, but this time he was writing to an individual named Gaius, not a church. After expressing his love for Gaius and his hope that Gaius was healthy, John praised Gaius for his faithful service to the church. Then John warned Gaius about a man named Diotrephes who refused to acknowledge John's authority and who prohibited the members in the church from reaching out to strangers. Also, John commended another man named Demetrius who was a good example to the church of walking in the truth. John then closed the letter by indicating that he hoped he would be able to see Gaius soon.

Jude (written approximately 65 CE): Supposedly written by one of Jesus' brothers, this short letter contains a harsh criticism of false teachers who had arisen within the Christian community. Comparing the false teachers in his day to wicked people in the Old Testament, Jude made the case that all wicked, regardless of the time period in which they lived, would be destroyed by God.

Scholars have noted that Jude's attack against wickedness is similar to what is stated in the second chapter of 2 Peter. The similarities include the following elements:

Jude		2 Peter[9]
4	godless men denying God	2:1
6	angels kept in darkness	2:4
7	destruction of Sodom	2:6
18	scoffers in the last day	3:3

Due to their interpretation of the above similarities, some scholars contend that whoever wrote the book of Jude did so based on similar passages in 2nd Peter.

Concluding Comments on the General Letters

Most of the books in this section reflect two crises which early Christians faced. One crisis was that of persecution. Several of the letters reflect anxiety concerning oppression that had come upon the church, mostly via the Roman Empire. Therefore, the writers of these letters, such as the Apostle Peter, wanted to encourage the believers to hold fast and not to give into the temptation either to take matters into their own hands and resist the persecution in a manner displeasing to God or to renounce their faith in order to save their physical lives. Rather, the believers were to recognize that they had an example of suffering to follow, that of Jesus himself, who endured the horror of the crucifixion even though he had done nothing to deserve it.

Another crisis the church had faced was the rise of false teachers. Several of the General Letters demonstrate a concern that some had entered into the church in order to mislead the believers. Therefore, the authors of the General Letters, such as the author of Jude, exhorted the believers to be aware of the false teachers and to avoid them. Their pathway led to destruction of the faith. Instead, believers were reminded to follow the teachings of the apostles carefully, because they were representatives of Jesus himself.

With this chapter on the General Letters coming to a close, it would be reasonable for a reader to assume that the genre of letter has been

---

[9] Kistemaker noted these similarities and many others in his book *Peter and Jude* (Grand Rapids: Baker Book House, 1987) (see page 357).

fully covered and that there are no further letters to consider in the New Testament. However, the last book of the Bible, the book of Revelation, also has several letters in its first few chapters. Also, Revelation has another connection to the General Letters in that the two main crises faced by the church according to the General Letters were also a concern for the author of Revelation, as is demonstrated in the next chapter.

Chapter Eleven
The Book of Revelation

AS the last book of the New Testament, the book of Revelation is not only the capstone of this section of the Bible, but it is also the final document in the Bible. Because it is the final book of the Bible and it appears to address issues concerning the end of time, it has become the focus of extraordinary attention. Numerous books have been written about the events of the end times based on interpretations of the book of Revelation. Furthermore, convinced that this book provides a blue print for how events will unfold at the end of the age, influential Christian preachers have attempted to persuade their audiences that they can predict aspects of the future based on their knowledge of the book of Revelation. Similarly, some conservative scholars contend that this document must speak beyond its time, because the writer of this book, the Apostle John, was empowered to envision the future via divine revelation. Those coming from this perspective contend that believers need to know exactly how the world is going to end, so that they can be prepared.

However, critical scholars contend that this is not the best approach to this complex book. They maintain that rather than being a book about the end of time, this book is focused on the situation of the church at the end of the first century CE. Pointing to images in Revelation that seem to be reflections of various aspects of ancient Roman culture, scholars coming from this perspective contend that the main purpose of Revelation was to encourage Christians in the first century to stand firm during a time of horrible persecution. While Christians in later periods of church history found comfort in this book, it was not written to them. The book of Revelation, according to this perspective, is a first century document that has little relevance for predicting the future.

Avoiding the debate about whether or not the book is future or past oriented, other scholars contend it is best to focus on the literary form of Revelation. As a book of apocalyptic literature, the purpose of the book was to encourage believers to endure during the cruelty of an oppressive regime whenever it might be in power—past, present, or future.

Authorship of Revelation

The debate over the authorship of Revelation is not a modern development, but it stretches back to the early church. In his comments on the canonization of the books of the New Testament, an early church historian named Eusebius indicated that the church was initially undecided about whether or not the book of Revelation should be included in the New Testament.[1] Some felt that it might have been written by a false teacher named Cerinthus, and therefore, it should not be considered authentic. However, other authorities in the church, including Eusebius, maintained that the Apostle John wrote this book during a time of forced exile on the island of Patmos, located next to the southwest coast of Asia Minor. According to the opening of the book of Revelation and according to church tradition, the Apostle John had been forced into exile by the Romans who, led by the Emperor Domitian, were attempting to suppress the church in the mid 90s CE. Hence, conservative scholars are comfortable with the idea that John, the youngest apostle who wrote the Gospel of John and the three letters of John, also wrote the book of Revelation.

Critical scholars disagree for two main reasons. First, they contend that it is unlikely that the Apostle John would have been alive in the 90s. Even if John was only a teenager during Jesus' ministry, he would have been at least 75 years old by the time Revelation was written. Given that people generally did not live that long in the first century CE and that the lives of Christians were particularly hard due to persecution, these scholars contend John would not have lived long enough to have written this book. Another reason certain scholars argue against John being the author is that they believe the genre of this book called for a hero of the faith to be the central character regardless of whether or not that person was still alive at the time. Hence, whoever wrote the book of Revelation

---

[1] Eusebius' comments can be found at http://www.ntcanon.org/Eusebius.html.

needed an authoritative figure such as John to receive the revelation that was the basis for the book. It was just a part of the literary form.

Content and Literary Form of Revelation

Regardless of what one chooses to believe about the authorship of the book of Revelation, one thing is clear. This book is very difficult to understand. One of the reasons it is hard to interpret is that it combines two literary forms: letters and apocalyptic literature (see comments below). Moreover, the content of this book is difficult to embrace because many of the images within the book are other worldly, as supernatural forces of good and evil war against each other while humans are caught in the middle.

After giving a brief statement about the author of the book, in the first chapter of the book of Revelation, Jesus is described in exalted terms. As the universal ruler of the kings of the earth and the head of the church, Jesus has great authority. He corrects the church and the world by sending plagues upon the earth. Moreover, the time will come when Jesus will take control of the earth. He will return and completely destroy the forces of evil.

In chapters 2 and 3, the literary form shifts from apocalyptic to a letter format, as seven churches were selected to receive guidance from the exalted Jesus. In each of the letters, Jesus commented briefly on some aspect of his authority, praised the church for what it was doing right, corrected the church concerning anything it was doing wrong, warned it of dire consequences should the people in the church refuse to obey, and promised the congregants a reward if they chose to obey.

There were three main issues of concern expressed in the letters. First, some of the churches were becoming apathetic. No longer passionate about their beliefs, they were drifting away from the faith. Second, some of the churches were being misled by false teachers. Because the church grew rapidly in the first century, certain individuals saw an opportunity to insert themselves as leaders in the church, but they were not true believers. They were more focused on exalting themselves and gaining financial benefits from the believers than they were interested in the well being of believers. Third, some of the churches were facing severe persecution. The Roman government felt that the Christians were a threat to the stability of the Empire, because Christians were worshipping Jesus as their king, not the Roman Emperor. Therefore, Christians were being arrested, taken to jail, tortured, and killed.

The chapters following the letters return to the apocalyptic literary form. As was noted in "Chapter Six", apocalyptic literature features a hero of the faith, supernatural revelation via an angel, the view that the future is pre-determined, and that hope for a better tomorrow must be deferred to the next life. All of these features are evident within the book of Revelation. As was noted above, the Apostle John is the hero of faith who received the revelation from God. While some of the revelation John received was via visions and hearing God speak, significant portions of the book of Revelation were given to John by angels who served Jesus. Concerning the fatalistic component, the book of Revelation clearly indicates that believers have very little choice about the future. The forces of evil have set in motion a series of events that will have drastic consequences for the believers, and there is nothing the believers can do about it. Some of them will go to prison, some of them will be tortured, and some will be killed. All the believers can do is stand firm in their faith until they pass from this world into the next. It is at this point that the believers should have hope, because in the next world evil will not be tolerated. The forces of evil will be judged and thrown into the lake of fire.

Between the time of the end of the first century CE and the end of the world, the believers can expect the war between good and evil to continue. From Revelation chapter 4 through chapter 20, the war between good and evil is presented in graphic terms. In heaven, the forces of good, including God on the throne, encourage the believers to stand firm and to understand that the plagues that come upon the earth are God's way to affirm that God is ultimately in control of earth's destiny. After a scene from heaven is given, the next scene is that of earth's response. The kings of the earth do not repent when the plagues come, nor do the forces of evil back down. Rather, as the book unfolds, the forces of evil become more intense as the plagues increase.

In a desperate attempt to overthrow God, the devil (the great dragon) leads his forces in an attack against heaven.

The Devil Attacks Heaven

The devil and his forces are met in the air by God's army, led by Michael the archangel, and the forces of evil are driven back.

Having lost this key battle, the devil intensifies his efforts on earth as he attempts to solidify his hold on humanity. This is bad news for believers, because the devil attempts to force them to give up their testimony through horrific persecution. In an attempt to bolster the believers, God sends messages to them supernaturally—they must hold on until the end.

The war between good and evil finally comes to a head when Jesus descends from heaven to fight the devil. They meet on a battlefield, and Jesus dispatches the devil easily with a word. However, the devil is not destroyed at that point but is only bound for 1000 years. According to Revelation chapter 20, John then sees the devil being arrested and sent to prison:

> Then I saw an angel coming down from heaven, holding in his hand the key to the bottomless pit and a great chain. He seized the dragon, that ancient serpent, who is the Devil and Satan, and bound him for a thousand years, and threw him into the pit, and locked and sealed it over him, so that he would deceive the nations no more, until the thousand years were ended.[2]

During this time period, martyred believers are raised from the dead, so that they can reign with Jesus on earth for one thousand years. At the end of that time, Satan is released, and one more time, he deceives the people of the world and leads them into battle against God's people. However, this time he will not survive. He will be defeated, bound, and thrown into the lake of fire.

Immediately after his demise, all of the people who have lived upon the earth are brought before God and judged according to their deeds as recorded in books kept by God and according to what is indicated in the "book of life". Those whose names are written in the book of life are allowed to enter into the new heaven and earth,

---

[2] Rev 20:1-3.

as described in Revelation chapters 21 and 22, but those whose names are not in the book of life are condemned to the lake of fire.

In the new heaven and earth, the pain and suffering in this world will be eliminated, as God dwells among his people. Moreover, the tree of life, last seen in the book of Genesis, reappears on the new earth, and God's people can freely come and eat from it, as described by John:

> Then the angel showed me the river of the water of life, bright as crystal, flowing from the throne of God and of the Lamb through the middle of the street of the city. On either side of the river is the tree of life with its twelve kinds of fruit, producing its fruit each month; and the leaves of the tree are for the healing of the nations.[3]

The book of Revelation then closes with John's exhortation to his readers to pay attention to what he has written. Those who listen will receive a blessing, but those who attempt to add to or take away from his words will be cursed. Hence, just as the first book of the Bible opened with a reference to the tree of life and a warning, so concludes the last book of the Bible.

Concluding Comments on Revelation

Throughout the book of Revelation, John alternately encouraged and warned his readers, as he urged them not to abandon their faith. Even though they are suffering horrific persecution and the forces of evil seem to be in control of earth, believers should not give up, because ultimately God will win in the end, destroying unbelievers and raising believers from the dead unto eternal life. Hence, if the believers hold on to their faith, they can look forward to an eternity of peace and joy, residing in a new heaven and earth in which God is continually present.

---

[3] Rev 22:1-2.

While the book of Revelation points toward a new creation, it does not lose sight of the journey that believers face and the suffering that they have to go through in this world. Therefore, Revelation echoes the larger story of the Bible, a story that is commented on more fully in the final chapter of this textbook.

Chapter Twelve
The Bible and Theology

AFTER having considered the main ideas of all of the books of the Bible and their accompanying literary forms as presented in this textbook, a reader of the Bible might legitimately wonder if the Bible is simply an anthology of loosely related religious books. Given the range of religious ideas present within the Bible, a reader could ask the question: Does the Bible have themes connecting the 66 books together as a literary whole or are the books so distinct that it isn't possible to even use the phrase "biblical themes" or "biblical theology"?[1]

Different Approaches to Biblical Theology

The answer to that question depends on which scholar responds. Generally scholars can be divided into three camps. One group of scholars maintains that it isn't possible to pull ideas from the various books and literary types and connect them together concerning such themes as God, sin, and salvation. Rather, they contend each book of the Bible must be examined separately. Hence, while it is not appropriate to write about themes of the Bible as a whole, it is appropriate to write about the concept of God as presented in the book of Genesis or as reflected in Paul's letter to the Romans. Scholars from this perspective do not believe the Bible as a whole presents a coherent picture of any religious concept, but rather, each book of the Bible presents a variation on religious themes.

A second group of scholars contends that it is possible to connect themes from biblical books together, but only within the context of each testament. Hence, it is appropriate to write about themes of the Old Testament or themes of the New Testament, but it is not appropriate to

---

[1] The word "theology" is based on two Greek words, *theos* which means "God" and *logos* which means word. In English usage, theology is used in reference to the study of God specifically or to the study of religious ideas generally. For the purposes of this chapter, theology is used in the second sense.

connect ideas across the testaments. The perspective of these scholars is that the two testaments reflect the religious experiences of two very different faith communities, one Jewish and the other Christian. Moreover, since the early Christians believed that the covenant they abided by superseded and replaced the covenant God made with the Jews, the New Testament contains polemical commentary deconstructing ideas within the Old Testament. Therefore, religious ideas from the two testaments cannot and should not be combined.

A third group of scholars contends that while the distinct elements of each book and each testament need to be honored, it is possible to connect ideas from all of the books of the Bible to each other. These scholars believe that since all of the books have gone through a process of selection and canonization, the books are no longer circulating independently of each other, but they are placed next to each other in a particular order, thereby creating a literary unit that has been in existence for at least 1600 years. As such, those who read through the Bible cannot help but to synthesize ideas from the various books in the Bible. Once Genesis has been read, information from that book influences how a reader will encounter other books of the Bible, regardless of the literary form of the book or the testament in which the book is located. The fact that these books have been placed together is a historical reality which cannot be ignored, irrespective of how those books ended up being placed into the same collection.

Another Option: Meta-narrative

While each of the above positions on the concept of biblical theology contributes significantly to the discussion about biblical theology, the perspective of this book is that none of them are the best approach when it comes to commenting on religious concepts reflected in the various books of the Bible. Rather, it is the perspective here that while there are various literary forms present throughout the Bible, ultimately the Bible tells a larger story—a meta-narrative—reflecting the experiences and understandings of religious communities which were counter-cultural in terms of their view of God and human nature. In the midst of societies which believed there were many deities, both early Jews and Christians believed in one God who created all things. Moreover, both communities were persecuted periodically for their beliefs. Jews were oppressed by several powerful nations, some of which attempted to force them to worship idols. Christians faced persecution at the hands of the Romans, who tortured and killed them. Yet, as similar as these two communities were, they also had very different ideas about how to relate to God. So the story of the Bible is one that has distinct chapters reflecting how characters in the story had different points of view about the same issue. In the commentary below, an attempt is made to demonstrate the consistencies and the tensions within the biblical story concerning four main themes reflected in both testaments.

Major Themes of the Bible

While theologians write extensively about a number of biblical themes such as sin, salvation, the church, and the end times, this text focuses on four themes that appear fairly consistently in both testaments.

God's Reign on Earth: In both the Old and the New Testaments, God is the protagonist around which the action of the narrative takes place. God attempts to establish a presence on earth, so that God's kingdom or God's kingly rule would be evident to all people. While God could and periodically did unleash judgment upon the earth as a reminder to people that God was still in charge, the primary method God used to establish his kingdom was through the obedience of selected individuals who were willing to sacrifice everything to follow God.

In the Old Testament, God selected Abraham and Sarah as the couple through whom God would begin to establish the nation of Israel, which was to be a kingdom of priests, an example to the world of a holy nation reflecting God's grace and justice. Later after Abraham's descendants were slaves in Egypt, God called Moses to bring the Israelites out of slavery, and then, God called Joshua to lead them into the Promised Land. Once the Israelites settled into the Promised Land, God corrected the Israelites when they were disobedient. Throughout the Old Testament, God interacted with the Israelites through prophets who reminded the Israelites that they needed to obey God by keeping the Law of Moses. Time and again, God intervened, correcting the Israelites, bringing them back from the brink of assimilation into the religious culture of their time. Israel, as God's chosen nation, had a mission to accomplish as reflected in the comments of the prophet Isaiah in the 8th century BCE:

> In days to come the mountain of the LORD's house shall be established as the highest of the mountains, and shall be raised above the hills; all the nations shall stream to it. Many peoples shall come and say, 'Come let us go up to the mountain of the LORD, to the house of the God of Jacob; that he may teach us his ways and that we may walk in his paths.' For out of Zion shall go forth instruction, and the word of the LORD from Jerusalem. He shall judge between the nations, and shall arbitrate for many peoples; they shall beat their swords into plowshares, and their spears into pruning hooks; nation shall not lift up sword against nation, neither shall they learn war any more.[2]

In the New Testament, God continues as the main character, but the story shifts in terms of how God chooses to reach people. While God still desires to change the world, the focus shifts from God's utilization of prophets to the belief that one man is the leader through whom all can relate to God. According to the New Testament, God sent his son into the world to die for the sins of humanity, so that all those who believe would be saved. Upon entering into this relationship with God, the believers become a light to the world, promoting God's kingdom among the nations, as reflected in the following New Testament passages:

> You are the salt of the earth; but if salt has lost its taste, how can its saltiness be restored? It is no longer good for anything, but is thrown out and trampled under foot. You are the light of the world. A city built on a hill cannot be hid. No one after

---

[2] Isa 2:2-4.

lighting a lamp puts it under the bushel basket, but on the lampstand, and it gives light to all in the house. In the same way, let your light shine before others, so that they may see your good works and give glory to your Father in heaven.[3]

All this is from God, who reconciled us to himself through Christ, and has given us the ministry of reconciliation; that is, in Christ God was reconciling the world to himself, not counting their trespasses against them, and entrusting the message of reconciliation to us. So we are ambassadors for Christ, since God is making his appeal through us; we entreat you on behalf of Christ, be reconciled to God.[4]

Like living stones, let yourselves be built into a spiritual house, to be a holy priesthood, to offer spiritual sacrifices acceptable to God through Jesus Christ.[5]

While there is a significant tension between the two pathways to God as presented in the Old and New Testaments (see further commentary below), a comparison of God in the Old Testament with God in the New Testament demonstrates that in both testaments God works through key leaders to draw humans to himself, so that those who believe in God can become God's representatives in the world, spreading the news that God cares for this world and desires that it be filled with justice and peace.

Human Choice: While some of the biblical characters promote God's kingdom on earth, others function as antagonists who work against God's purposes. The antagonists choose to disobey God and God's representatives, living lives of disobedience that are harmful to those around them. Callously ignoring the hurting around them, they pretend there is no God and that they have no accountability for their actions. They make the world a darker place morally, spiritually, socially, and economically.

---

[3] Matt 5:13-16.
[4] 2 Cor 5:18-20.
[5] 1 Pet 2:5.

In the Old Testament, many of the kings of Israel functioned as antagonists, including King Manasseh who sacrificed children to the god Molech. Because Manasseh was so perverted and unjust, God decided that Judah, the nation ruled by Manasseh, would be destroyed. Manasseh's disobedience not only hurt him and his family, but it contributed to the destruction of a nation.

In the New Testament, an example of an antagonist is Judas Iscariot. One of the original twelve disciples of Jesus, Judas secretly was stealing from the funds that the disciples and Jesus were using to support themselves and to help the poor. Realizing that delivering Jesus over to the authorities was worth a great deal of money, Judas decided to betray Jesus, resulting in Jesus' arrest, torture, and crucifixion. Judas not only contributed to the death of a caring person who had been making other people's lives better, but Judas ultimately could not cope with his own treacherous act. After Jesus was arrested, Judas killed himself.

In contrast to the antagonists, a few biblical characters (often after dramatic religious experiences or trials) decided to submit to God, seeking to serve God by helping others. These characters humbly followed God's leaders, even if that meant they were persecuted for their efforts. When they saw someone who was hurting, they did what they could to address that person's needs. Their actions clearly made the world a better place for everyone else.

An example of a proponent in the Old Testament is Joseph. As was noted in "Chapter Three", Joseph was the second youngest of twelve brothers. Because Joseph was favored by his father Jacob, Joseph was hated by his brothers, who sold Joseph into slavery when they had the chance. Years later, when the brothers were looking for food in order to survive a famine, they encountered Joseph. But he was no longer a teenager unable to defend himself. Rather, he was the right hand man of Pharaoh, the most powerful king on earth at the time. While a reader might reasonably expect that Joseph would use his power to get revenge on his brothers, Joseph refused to do so. Instead Joseph forgave them and allowed them and their families to settle in Egypt, so that they could survive the famine. If Joseph had not been so gracious, the Hebrews might not have grown into a mighty nation which eventually settled in the Promised Land.

An example of a proponent in the New Testament is Jesus. Like Joseph, Jesus was persecuted unjustly. At a time when his people were being influenced to go to war with Rome, Jesus chose to present a new view of God and God's Kingdom. Contending that violently overthrowing Roman rule was not the pathway to true freedom, Jesus commanded his followers to love their enemies. Moreover, he called his disciples to live lives of self sacrifice, putting the needs of others ahead of their own. Although he had very little in terms of financial resources, Jesus shared what he did have, caring for the poor and those who were hurting. His influence was so overwhelming that his followers contended that death could not hold him after he had been crucified. Based on their view that Jesus had been raised from the dead, Jesus' followers contended that through Jesus' death and resurrection a new pathway had been opened up to God; a new covenant had been established.

Covenant: Both the Old and the New Testaments focus on the concept of covenant as the key to understanding God's relationship with humans. As was noted in "Chapter Two", a covenant was a treaty or agreement between two parties that had a conflict. It was a way to settle the conflict, so that there would be peace between the parties. In the Bible, three parts of the covenant were emphasized, including the *promises* of the more powerful party to be helpful to the weaker party, *obligations* on the weaker party to be respectful to the more powerful one, and a *sign* of the covenant.

In the Old Testament, several covenants were made. First, God made a covenant with Noah and his family. God's promise to Noah was that God would not destroy the world by flood again. Noah's obligations included producing children, not eating blood, and not committing murder. The sign of the covenant was the rainbow. The essence of this covenant was that God would allow the world to continue. Second, God made a covenant with Abraham and Sarah. God's promises to Abraham and Sarah included many descendants, a land of their own, a great nation, and a blessing to others through them. Their obligations in return involved following God wherever God led them, having great faith in God regardless of the circumstance or test that might come upon them, and circumcising their male children, which was also the sign of the covenant. The essence of this covenant was that God was going to establish a people through whom God would bless the rest of the nations. Third, God made a covenant with the Israelites through the mediation of Moses. After proving his care for them by delivering them from slavery in Egypt, God offered the Israelites a covenant which would bind them to God and God to them. They agreed to the deal. The promises of God in this covenant included great blessings of prosperity, peace, and fertility. In return, the Israelites were given the Ten Commandments along with over 600 other commandments, including obligations involving sacrifices for sin, what food may or may not be eaten, a civil code, feast laws, relationship standards, and hygiene regulations. The sign of this covenant was the Ark of the covenant, a small chest which contained the two stone tablets upon which were written the Ten Commandments. The essence of this covenant is that it was the constitution for a holy nation that would be an example to the rest of the world.

While the first three covenants in the Old Testament are located in the Pentateuch, the fourth covenant is located in one of the Historical Books. According to 2 Samuel chapter 7, King David was given a covenant by God that included God's promise to extend the Davidic dynasty into eternity, the obligation of the kings of Judah to obey God, and the sign of a Davidic king sitting on the throne in the palace in Jerusalem. This covenant became the foundation for two types of prophetic texts. One type focuses on foretelling a future great Davidic king, a Messiah, who would guide his people into a time of peace and prosperity. Another type of prophecy is more general, foretelling of a time when God would make a different covenant with the Jews, not based on a national obedience, but based on individual obedience. No longer would all of the Jews be punished due to the sins of the king of Judah, but rather, each person would be judged based on his or her own actions. The result would be a "Messianic age" in which every believer in God would be accountable for their own actions.

In the New Testament, some aspects of the covenants mentioned in the Old Testament are upheld and expanded, while others are discarded. Concerning what is discarded, in the letters of Paul, Paul contended that the Mosaic Covenant as a whole was no longer valid. Even though Jesus seemed to uphold the Law of Moses in his teaching, in several of Paul's letters, Paul contended that this covenant was too legalistic and that it was preempted by the Abrahamic Covenant, which Paul maintained was the basis for a new covenant that God had made with all of humanity, Jew and Gentile. As was noted above, this new covenant was based on the belief that Jesus' death at the hands of the Romans was the atoning sacrifice for the sins of the world. Therefore, in Paul's perspective everyone who has faith in Jesus will be saved. Interestingly, even though Paul utilized the Abrahamic Covenant to support Paul's view that believers in Jesus were simply following Abraham's example of faith in God, it is important to note that Paul did not uphold all aspects of the Abrahamic Covenant. For example, Paul rejected the obligation of circumcision, even though that was the sign of the covenant with Abraham.

Along with connecting the New Testament covenant with the faith aspect of the Abrahamic Covenant, New Testament writers also connected it to both the Noahic and the Davidic Covenants as well. The covenant in the New Testament was connected to the Noahic Covenant in that the prohibition against eating blood as commanded in the Noahic Covenant was also required of Gentile Christians according to the Jerusalem Council (see "Chapter Nine" commentary). Concerning the connection to the Davidic Covenant, many of the authors of New Testament documents contended that Jesus came in the line of David, and hence, they build on prophetic texts which foretell of a coming great king, the Messiah, who will save the world (at least according to the interpretations in the New Testament).

Given the disparity between the Mosaic Covenant with its numerous laws in the Old Testament and the covenant in the New Testament with its emphasis on faith in Jesus, there is a significant tension in the biblical story when it comes to the theme of covenant. While the theme definitely is in both testaments, the direction that the New Testament writers went with this theme ultimately created the context for a split between early Christianity and Rabbinic Judaism.

Based on their interpretation of the Old Testament (which they referred to as Scripture), the Rabbis who led the Jews after the destruction of the Second Temple in 70 CE chose the Mosaic Covenant as the covenant for their people in light of the prophetic texts calling for individual responsibility. Over time, they built on this covenant through commentary on the Torah, which they called the Talmud.

In contrast, the early Christians chose the Davidic Covenant as the basis for the covenant they were proclaiming to both Jew and Gentile. Contending that Jesus was the Messiah in the line of David sent to save the world, the Christians felt that the Mosaic Covenant and the commandment to be circumcised according to the Abrahamic Covenant were too difficult for the Gentiles to keep and that it was not necessary to keep them in order to have a relationship with God.

So the Christian solution was to reclassify older sacred texts primarily focused on the Mosaic Covenant as "the Old Testament" and to classify newer sacred texts focused on the covenant through faith in Jesus as the "New Testament". While the New Testament built on certain aspects of the Old, it created a new understanding of the role of the Messiah and the pathway to God. Conversely, the Jewish solution was to reject the New Testament, preferring to keep the 39 books of the Old Testament as the only Bible.

Hence, in many ways, the biblical theme of covenant created a story with two alternative endings with one focused on demonstrating faith in God through keeping the Law and the other on coming to God through faith in Jesus. The question is: where does each one lead?

Eternal Life: While some scholars contend that the theme of eternal life is not emphasized until the New Testament, there is significant evidence that in both the Old and the New Testaments, living forever is something biblical characters hoped to gain. However God was not willing to allow everyone to have it.

In the Old Testament, eternal life is first presented as something that could be gained in this world. In Genesis chapters 2 and 3, Adam and Eve were placed in the Garden of Eden, which had the "Tree of Life". However, when Adam and Eve disobeyed God by eating of the forbidden fruit, they were driven out of the garden, because God did not want them to eat from the Tree of Life and live forever as rebels in God's kingdom.

While humans could no longer live forever on the earth, that didn't mean that humans couldn't live forever in heaven. The concept of heaven is mostly evident in prophetic passages in the Old Testament. For example, according to the book of Isaiah, Isaiah saw God sitting on a throne in heaven, surrounded by heavenly beings. It is important to note that Isaiah's vision of heaven appeared to him while Isaiah was standing in the Temple. Hence, heaven is not something that is up in the sky, but rather, it is a world in a parallel dimension in the universe. The question is: how can humans get there?

In Genesis chapter 5, one of the biblical characters named Enoch was described as one who "walked with God; then he was no more, because God took him."[6] While some scholars note that this passage doesn't specifically mention Enoch going to heaven, others contend that it supports the concept of a spiritual world beyond earth. There are other passages that support this contention. For example, in Exodus there is a reference to a "book" that God keeps in which are written the names of those who serve God.[7] The implication is that God is keeping a record of those who please him and those who don't for future reference. Another example is found in a passage in 1 Samuel in which King Saul goes to a witch and has her bring up the spirit of the Prophet Samuel from the dead.[8] Not only was the witch successful in her endeavors, but also Samuel was able to speak to Saul and remind Saul what Samuel said while Samuel was still alive. Clearly, Samuel was in another world, retained his memory, and could still communicate to others. Yet another example is that of the prophet Elijah being taken up to heaven in a

---

[6] Gen 5:24.
[7] Exod 32:32.
[8] 1 Sam 28.

chariot of fire while he was talking to Elisha, the prophet who would replace Elijah:

> When they had crossed, Elijah said to Elisha, "Tell me what I may do for you, before I am taken from you." Elisha said, "Please let me inherit a double share of your spirit." He responded, "You have asked a hard thing; yet, if you see me as I am being taken from you, it will be granted you; if not, it will not." As they continued walking and talking, a chariot of fire and horses of fire separated the two of them, and Elijah ascended in a whirlwind into heaven. Elisha kept watching and crying out, "Father, father! The chariots of Israel and its horsemen!" But when he could no longer see him, he grasped his own clothes and tore them in two pieces.[9]

While the above passages demonstrate that proponents of God in the Old Testament could reach heaven and be with God, there are other passages which indicate that the separation between God's dimension and the dimension in which the earth resides will someday be replaced by a new creation designed for those who followed God on earth. According to the book of Isaiah, God told Isaiah that God was going to recreate the world: "For I am about to create new heavens and a new earth; the former things shall not be remembered or come to mind."[10]

Interestingly, the biblical story as reflected in the Old Testament reconnects with the story in the New Testament concerning the theme of eternal life. While the testaments are in tension about how people can gain eternal life (see commentary above), they seem to agree that humans can achieve eternal life with God, first with God in heaven, and then at some future point in a new creation that replaces the current earth. For example, in the New Testament, believers were encouraged to hold fast during times of persecution, because they were told that eternal life in heaven awaited them. One of the clearest expressions of this idea is found in the Gospel of John: "For God so loved the world that he gave

---

[9] 2 Kgs 2:9-12.
[10] Isa 65:17.

his only Son, so that everyone who believes in him may not perish but may have eternal life."[11]

However, unlike what is found in the Old Testament in which the eternal relationship between God and humans is direct, in the New Testament eternal life is not available apart from the Christian concept of the "Second Coming". This concept includes the belief that at a future date Jesus will come from heaven and gather his followers, raising them from the dead. This idea is supported in the writings of Paul, as demonstrated in the following passage:

> But we do not want you to be uninformed, brothers and sisters, about those who have died, so that you may not grieve as others do who have no hope. For since we believe that Jesus died and rose again, even so, through Jesus, God will bring with him those who have died. For this we declare to you by the word of the Lord, that we who are alive, who are left until the coming of the Lord, will by no means precede those who have died. For the Lord himself, with a cry of command, with the archangel's call and with the sound of God's trumpet, will descend from heaven, and the dead in Christ will rise first. Then we who are alive, who are left, will be caught up in the clouds together with them to meet the Lord in the air; and so we will be with the Lord forever.[12]

After being affirmed in the Day of Judgment that their names are indeed recorded in the book of life, believers will one day reside with God forever in a new heaven and earth according to the book of Revelation:

---

[11] John 3:16.
[12] 1 Thess 4:13-17.

> Then I saw a new heaven and a new earth; for the first heaven and the first earth had passed away, and the sea was no more. And I saw the holy city, the new Jerusalem, coming down out of heaven from God, prepared as a bride adorned for her husband...I saw a temple in the city, for its temple is the Lord God the Almighty and the Lamb. And the city has no need of sun or moon to shine on it, for the glory of God is its light, and its lamp is the Lamb. The nations will walk by its light, and the kings of the earth will bring their glory into it.[13]

Hence, in spite of significant differences between the two testaments concerning how believers can come to God, they seem to agree that the followers of God on earth do not cease to exist when their physical bodies die. Rather, their souls continue to have a relationship with God, and eventually they are given new bodies which will reside in a new heaven and earth in which God will continually be present.

Concluding Thoughts

In the opening chapter of this book, it was noted that the Bible is a difficult book to understand, because it was written a long time ago by ancient Israelites and Christians who lived in a world much different from the contemporary world. Moreover, it contains 66 books written over a lengthy period of time, and these books were written in several different literary forms or genres that are quite distinct from contemporary literature. Furthermore, the Bible tells a complicated story about God, who attempts to change the world through the obedience of those who choose to follow God. Hence, a reader of the Bible has much to consider literarily, historically, and theologically.

Thankfully, contemporary biblical scholarship has narrowed the gap between the contemporary reader and the ancient text. Excellent English translations with helpful commentary on the meaning of the biblical text are readily available, and numerous other supporting secondary sources

---

[13] Rev 21:1-2, 22-24.

are available that help the reader to understand the cultural background, the literary forms, and the issues of authorship of the books of the Bible. What is necessary then to be a good student of the Bible is a commitment to study the text and the willingness to set aside the time necessary for the study to be effective.

While it is the hope of the author of this textbook that the student's journey through the Bible (as presented here) has been productive, there is also a hope that the journey won't end. There is much more that can be gained from reading the Bible. May all who decide to continue to study the Bible find a blessing in their efforts.

Appendices

and

Selected Bibliography

Appendix A
The Hebrew Alphabet

Hebrew Letter	Name of Letter	Pronunciation
א	*aleph*	no sound
ב	*bet*	b or v
ג	*gimmel*	g
ד	*dalet*	d
ה	*heh*	h
ו	*vav*	v
ז	*zayin*	z
ח	*khet*	kh
ט	*tet*	t
י	*yod*	y
כ	*kaph*	k or kh
ל	*lamed*	l
מ	*mem*	m
נ	*nun*	n
ס	*samek*	s
ע	*ayin*	no sound
פ	*pe*	p or ph
צ	*tsade*	tz
ק	*qoph*	q
ר	*resh*	r
ש	*sin & shin*	s & sh
ת	*tav*	t

Appendix B
The Greek Alphabet

Greek Letter	Name of Letter	Pronunciation
α	*alpha*	a
β	*beta*	b
γ	*gamma*	g
δ	*delta*	d
ϵ	*epsilon*	e
ζ	*zeta*	z
η	*eta*	ē
θ	*theta*	th
ι	*iota*	i
κ	*kappa*	k
λ	*lambda*	l
μ	*mu*	m
ν	*nu*	n
ξ	*xsi*	xs
ο	*omicron*	o
π	*pi*	p
ρ	*rho*	r
σ	*sigma*	s
τ	*tau*	t
υ	*upsilon*	u
φ	*phi*	ph
χ	*chi*	ch
ψ	*psi*	ps
ω	*omega*	ō

Appendix C

Old Testament Timeline

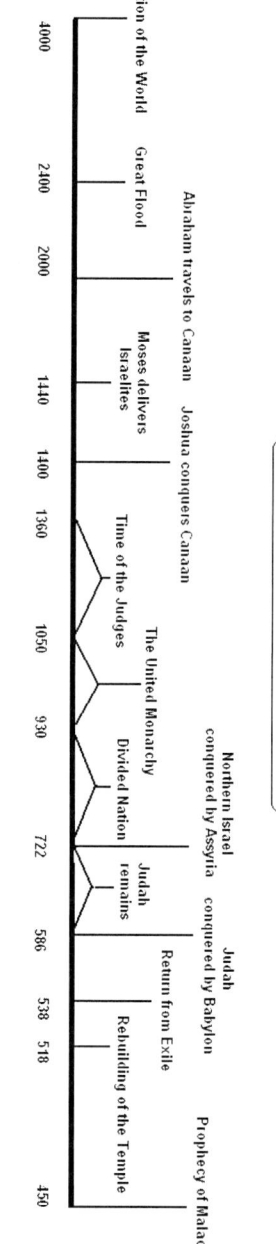

All dates are "Before the Common Era" (BCE).

Appendix D
New Testament Timeline

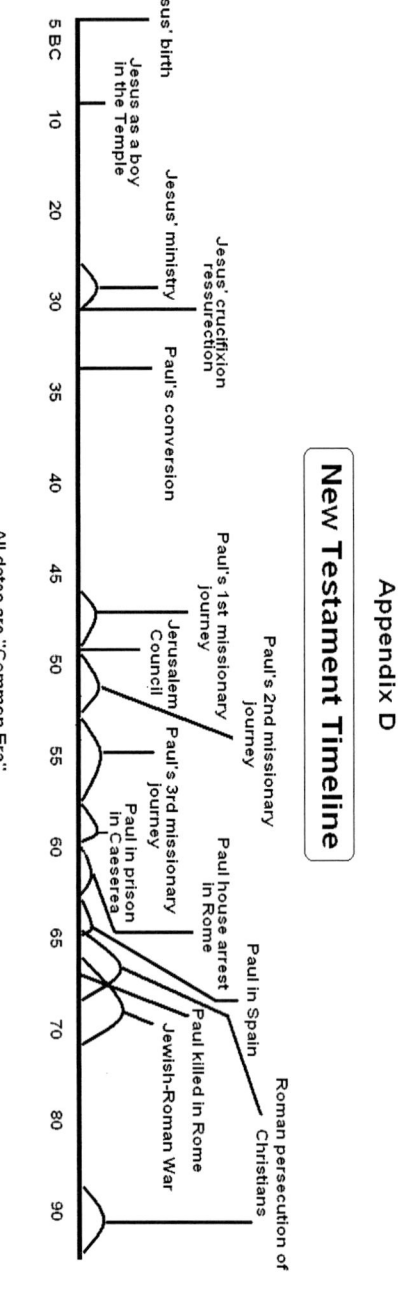

Selected Bibliography

Background of the Old Testament

Websites

On Ancient Assyria

http://www.aina.org/aol/link4.htm

On Ancient Babylon

http://www.bible-history.com/babylonia/

http://www.sacred-texts.com/ane/enuma.htm

http://www.wsu.edu/~dee/MESO/CODE.HTM

On Ancient Egypt

http://www.earthyfamily.com/Egypt/picts/chart.gif

On Ancient Sumer

http://www.ancienttexts.org/library/mesopotamian/gilgamesh/)

Books

Bright, John. *A History of Israel*. Philadelphia: Westminster, 1981.

Gordon, Cyrus and Gary Rendsburg. *The Bible and the Ancient Near East*. New York: W. W. Norton and Company, 1997.

Grant, Michael. *The History of Ancient Israel*. New York: Charles Scribner's Sons, 1984.

Hess, Richard. *Israelite Religions*. Grand Rapids: Baker, 2007.

King, Philip and L. Stager. *Life in Biblical Israel*. London: Westminster John Knox Press, 2001.

Leick, Gwendolyn. *The Babylonians*. London: Routledge, 2003.

Oakes, Lorna and Lucia Gahlin. *Ancient Egypt*. London: Hermes House, 2002.

Pritchard, James, ed. *The Ancient Near East: An Anthology of Texts and Pictures*. Princeton: Princeton University Press, 1958.

Redford, Donald. *Egypt, Canaan, and Israel in Ancient Times*. Princeton, New Jersey: Princeton University Press, 1992.

Shanks, Hershel, ed. *Ancient Israel*. Upper Saddle River, New Jersey: Prentice Hall, 1999.

The Bible Visual Resource Book. Ventura, California: Regal Books, 1989.

Background of the New Testament

Barnett, Paul. *Behind the Scenes of the New Testament*. Downers Grove, Illinois: Intervarsity Press, 1990.

Barrett, C.K. *The New Testament Background: Selected Documents*. San Francisco: Harper & Row, Pub., 1987.

Carcopino, Jerome. *Daily Life in Ancient Rome: The People and the City at the Height of the Empire*. Edited by Henry Rowell. Translated by E. Lorimer. New Haven, Connecticut: Yale University Press, 1940.

Filson, Floyd. *A New Testament History*. Philadelphia: Westminster Press, 1964.

Freedman, David, Gary Herion, David Graf, John Pleins, and Astrid Beck, eds. *Anchor Bible Dictionary*. 6 vols. New York: Doubleday, 1992.

Neusner, Jacob. *The Pharisees: Rabbinic Perspectives*. Hoboken, New Jersey: Ktav Publishing House, Inc., 1973.

Niswonger, Richard. *New Testament History*. Grand Rapids: Zondervan, 1988.

Schiffman, Lawrence. *From Text to Tradition: A History of Second Temple and Rabbinic Judaism.* Hoboken, New Jersey: Ktav Pub., 1991.

Thompson, J.A. *Handbook of Life in Bible Times*. Downers Grove, Illinois: Intervarsity Press, 1986.

Vermes, Geza. *The Dead Sea Scrolls in English*. Middlesex, England: Penguin Books Ltd, 1968.

Canonization and Formation of the Bible

Websites

http://www.bible-researcher.com/canon2.html

http://www.earlychristianwritings.com/muratorian.html

http://www.ntcanon.org/Eusebius.shtml

Books

Bruce, F. F. *The Canon of Scripture*. Downers Grove, Illinois: Intervarsity Press, 1988.

Cameron, Ron, ed. *The Other Gospels: The Non-Canonical Gospel Texts*. Philadelphia: The Westminster Press, 1982.

Elliot, J.K., ed. *The Apocryphal New Testament*. Oxford: Clarendon Press, 1993.

Ewert, David. *From Ancient Tablets to Modern Translations*. Grand Rapids: Zondervan, 1983.

Koch, Klaus. *The Growth of the Biblical Tradition*. Translated by S. Cupitt. New York: Charles Scribner's Sons, 1969.

Rowley, H. H. *The Growth of the Old Testament.* London: Hutchinson's House, 1950.

Weiser, Artur. *The Old Testament: Its Formation and Development*. New York: Association Press, 1961.

Commentaries on the Bible

Goldingay, John. *Old Testament Commentary Survey*. Madison, Wisconsin: Inter-varsity Christian Fellowship, 1981.

Kistemaker, Simon. *Exposition of the Epistles of Peter and of the Epistle of Jude.* Grand Rapids: Baker Book House, 1987.

Metzger, Bruce., et. al. eds. *Word Biblical Commentary Series*. Waco, Texas: Word Books, 1982f.

Tylenda, Joseph., et. al. eds. *Anchor Bible Commentary Series*. New York: Doubleday, 1970f.

Introductions to the Bible

Harris, Stephen. *Understanding the Bible*. New York: McGraw-Hill, 2007.

Hauer, Christian and William Young. *An Introduction to the Bible.* Upper Saddle River, New Jersey: Prentice Hall, 2008.

Literary Forms in the Bible

Alter, Robert. *The World of Biblical Literature.* New York: BasicBooks, 1992.

Anderson, B., and W. Harrelson, eds. *Israel's Prophetic Heritage.* New York: Harper & Row, 1962.

Baltzer, K. "Considerations Regarding the Office and Calling of the Prophet." *HTR* 61 (1968) 567-581.

Blenkinsopp, Joseph. Wisdom *and Law in the Old Testament: The Ordering of Life in Israel and Early Judaism.* Revised Edition. Oxford Bible Series Edited by P.R. Ackroyd and G.N. Stanton. Oxford: Oxford Univ. Press, 1995.

Callaway, Phillip. "Deut 21:18-21: Proverbial Wisdom and Law." *JBL* 103/3 (1984) 341-352.

Clements, R. *Prophecy and Tradition.* Atlanta: John Knox Press, 1975.

Craigie, Peter, Page Kelly, and Joel Drinkard, Jr. *Jeremiah 1-15. Word Biblical Commentary.* Vol. 26. Dallas, Texas: Word Books, Pub., 1991.

Davison, W. *The Wisdom-Literature of the Old Testament.* London: Charles Kelly, 1904.

Eissfeldt, O. "The Prophetic Literature." *The Old Testament and Modern Study: A Generation of Discovery and Research.* Edited by H. Rowley. Oxford: Clarendon Press, 1951.

Gabel, John, Charles Wheeler, and Anthony York. *The Bible as Literature*. Oxford: Oxford Univ. Press, 2000.

Hayes, John and Carl Holladay. *Biblical Exegesis*. Atlanta: John Knox Press, 1987.

Kaiser, Walter and Moises Silva. *An Introduction to Biblical Hermeneutics*. Grand Rapids: Zondervan, 1994.

Kent, Charles. *Israel's Laws and Legal Precedents*. Hodder and Stoughton, 1907.

Perdue, Leo, Bernard Scott, and William Wiseman, eds. *In Search of Wisdom: Essays in Memory of John G. Gammie*. Louisville, Kentucky: Westminster/John Knox Press, 1993.

Peterson, David, ed. *Prophecy in Israel: Search for an Identity*. Issues in Religion and Theology Series. Edited by Douglas Knight and Robert Morgan. Philadelphia: Fortress Press, 1987.

Robinson, T. *The Poetry of the Old Testament*. London: Gerald Duckworth & Co. Ltd., 1960.

Ryken, Leland. *How to Read the Bible as Literature*. Grand Rapids: Zondervan, 1984.

von Rad, Gerhard. *Wisdom in Israel*. Nashville: Abingdon Press, 1972.

Surveys of the Old Testament

Anderson, Berhhard. *Understanding the Old Testament*. Upper Saddle River, New Jersey: Prentice Hall, 2007.

Bandstra, Barry. *Reading the Old Testament*. Belmont, California: Wadsworth, 2009.

Bowley, James. *Introduction to the Hebrew Bible*. Upper Saddle River, New Jersey: Prentice Hall, 2008.

Brueggemann, Walter. *An Introduction to the Old Testament*. Louisville, Kentucky: Westminster John Knox Press, 2003.

Craigie, Peter. *The Old Testament*. Nashville: Abingdon Press, 1986.

Föhrer, Georg. *Introduction to the Old Testament*. Translated by D. Green. Nashville: Abingdon Press, 1968.

Harris, Stephen. *The Old Testament: An Introduction to the Hebrew Bible*. New York: McGraw-Hill, 2008.

Hill, Andrew and John Walton. *A Survey of the Old Testament*. Grand Rapids: Zondervan, 2000.

Tullock, John. *The Old Testament Story*. Upper Saddle River, New Jersey: Prentice Hall, 1999.

Young, Edward. *An Introduction to the Old Testament*. Grand Rapids: Eerdmans, 1958.

Surveys of the New Testament

Carson, D. A. and Douglas Moo. *An Introduction to the New Testament*. Grand Rapids: Zondervan, 2005.

Ehrman, Bart. *The New Testament*. Oxford: Oxford University Press, 2008.

Gundry, Robert. *A Survey of the New Testament*. Grand Rapids: Zondervan, 1970.

Guthrie, Donald. *New Testament Introduction*. London: Tyndale Press, 1965.

Johnson, Luke. *The Writings of the New Testament.* Philadelphia: Fortress Press, 1986.

Kümmel, Werner. *Introduction to the New Testament.* Translated by Howard Kee. Nashville: Abingdon Press, 1975.

Puskas, Charles. *An Introduction the New Testament.* Peabody, Massachusetts: Hendrickson Pub., 1989.

Scott, Ernest. *The Literature of the New Testament.* New York: Columbia University Press, 1936.

Selvidge, Marla. *Exploring the New Testament.* Upper Saddle River, New Jersey: Prentice Hall, 2003.

Spivey, Robert and D. Smith. *Anatomy of the New Testament.* New York: MacMillan Pub., 1974.

Tenney, Merrill. *New Testament Survey.* Grand Rapids: Eerdmans, 1961.

Thiessen, H. C. *Introduction to the New Testament.* Grand Rapids: Eerdmans, 1943.

Theology and the Bible

Bultmann, Rudolf. *Theology of the New Testament.* Translated by K. Grobel. New York: Charles Scribner's Sons, 1955.

Childs, Brevard. *Biblical Theology of the Old and New Testaments.* Minneapolis: Augsburg Fortress Press, 1992.

_____. *Old Testament Theology in a Canonical Context.* Philadelphia: Fortress Press, 1985.

Guthrie, Donald. *New Testament Theology.* Downers Grove, Illinois: Intervarsity Press, 1981.

House, Paul. *Old Testament Theology*. Downers Grove, Illinois: Intervarsity Press, 1998.

Morris, Leon. *New Testament Theology*. Grand Rapids: Zondervan, 1986.

Von Rad, Gerhard. *Old Testament Theology*. Translated by D. Stalker. New York: Harper and Row Pub., 1962.